STIR FRY COOKBOOK

Delicious Stir Fries for Quick Meals

(Everything From Chicken Stir Fry to Beef Stir Fry Cookbook)

Ruben Burchette

Published by Sharon Lohan

© **Ruben Burchette**

All Rights Reserved

Stir Fry Cookbook: Delicious Stir Fries for Quick Meals (Everything From Chicken Stir Fry to Beef Stir Fry Cookbook)

ISBN 978-1-990334-49-8

All rights reserved. No part of this guide may be reproduced in any form without permission in writing from the publisher except in the case of brief quotations embodied in critical articles or reviews.

Legal & Disclaimer

The information contained in this book is not designed to replace or take the place of any form of medicine or professional medical advice. The information in this book has been provided for educational and entertainment purposes only.

The information contained in this book has been compiled from sources deemed reliable, and it is accurate to the best of the Author's knowledge; however, the Author cannot guarantee its accuracy and validity and cannot be held liable for any errors or omissions. Changes are periodically made to this book. You must consult your doctor or get professional medical advice before using any of the suggested remedies, techniques, or information in this book.

Table of contents

Part 1 1
Introduction 2
Selecting The Equipment 4
Chapter 1: Pork Stir-Fry Recipes 5
1. Ginger-Lemon Pork 6
2. Spicy Black Bean Sauce Pork 8
3. Sticky Pork And Mange Tout 10
4. Pork With Lo Mein Noodles And Vegetables 12
5. Spicy Ground Pork With Cucumbers 15
6. Sweet And Sour Pork 18
7. Pork With Kale And Spring Onions 22
8. Caramelized Pork – Vietnamese 24
9. Spicy Pork 26
10. Pork And Pepper 27
11. Pork, Ginger, And Apple With Hoisin Sauce 31
Chapter 2: Poultry Stir-Fry Recipes 33
12. Szechuan/Sichuan Chicken 34
13. Ginger Chicken 36
14. Cashew Chicken Ding With Celery, Jicama (Mexican Turnip) And Red Bell Pepper 39
15. General Tso Chicken 43
16. Sichuan Kung Pao Chicken 48
17. Chicken With Oyster Sauce And Mushrooms 52

18. Honey Nut Chicken 56
19. Garden Chicken 58
20. Avocado Chicken 60
21. Orange Chicken 63
22. Duck With Ginger And Greens 65
Chapter 3: Stir-Fry Beef Recipes 67
23. Crispy Chili Beef 68
24. Beef And Black Bean 70
25. Beef With Chinese Broccoli 72
26. Beef With Snap Peas And Oyster Sauce 75
27. Chinese Pepper Steak 78
28. Quick Beef Recipe 80
29. Orange Zest Beef (Spicy) 82
30. Sesame Beef 85
31. Mongolian Beef And Spring Onions 87
32. Black Pepper Beef And Cabbage 90
33. Beef With Tangerine Sauce 92
Chapter 4: Marine Stir-Fry Recipes 95
34. Shrimp, Eggs And Garlic Chives 95
35. Bang Bang Chili Prawn 98
Conclusion 101
Part 2 102
Recipe 1: Potato Stir Fry 103
Recipe 2: Turkey With Cranberry Glaze 105
Recipe 3: Beef And Broccoli Stir Fry 107

Recipe 4: Tuna & Vegetable Stir Fry 109
Recipe 5: Beef And Noodle Stir Fry 111
Recipe 6: Stir Fry Shrimp With Garlic And Coriander 113
Recipe 7: Carrots With Pineapple Stir Fry.................. 115
Recipe 8: Stir Fried Lamb With Orange 117
Recipe 9: Chicken & Noodle And Oyster Mushroom Stir Fry.. 119
Recipe 10: Stir Fry Chili Cucumber 121
Recipe 11: Chicken Liver Stir Fry.............................. 123
Recipe 12: Stir Fry Fish With Ginger And Leek......... 125
Recipe 13: Chicken With Vegetables 127
Recipe 14: Stir Fried Greens..................................... 129
Recipe 15: Five Spiced Pork 131
Recipe 16: Stir Fried Ginger Chicken........................ 133
Recipe 17: Fruity Duck Stir Fry 135
Recipe 18: Stir Fried Cod With Mango 137
Recipe 19: Gingered Broccoli.................................... 139
Recipe 20: Vegetable Stir Fry................................... 141
Recipe 21: Green Bean Stir Fry 143
Recipe 22: Shrimp Stir Fry 145
Recipe 23: Green Chicken Stir Fry 147
Recipe 24: Sesame Lamb Stir Fry............................. 149
Recipe 25: Pork Caramel And Pineapple 151
Chinese Almond Chicken 153

Chinese Happy Family 154
Chow Mein With Chicken And Vegetables 156
Chrysanthemum Chicken 157
Citrus Chicken Stir Fry 159
Classic Pad Thai 161
Coconut Chicken Stir Fry 163
Crazy Chicken 164
Creamy Curried Chicken 166
Creamy Peanut Stir Fried Chicken 167
Curried Chicken 169
Curry Chicken And Vegetables 170
Curry Pineapple Fried Rice 172
Dak Galbi (Korean Spicy Chicken Stir Fry) 173
Delicious And Fast Chicken Curry 175
Denise's Peanut Chicken 176
Drunken Noodles 177
Easy Sweet And Sour Chicken 179
Easy Teriyaki Chicken Brown Rice Dinner 181
Easy And Spicy Thai Basil Chicken With Egg 182
Farmer's Market Corn Toss 184
Fast Sesame Chicken 185
Favorite Sweet And Sour Chicken 186
Fiery Pepper Chicken 188
Freezer Friendly Thai Chicken 190

Part 1

Introduction

Many chefs and moms all over the globe are embracing the art of stir-frying to create a dishy meal for the family or consumers in general. In the course of cooking, you will learn that this cooking technique involves cutting down of food into small pieces before cooking them rapidly with excess heat and little oil. The sequence of adding to the wok/pan considers putting first what will take longer to prepare and the ingredients needing shorter following later.

When the instructions direct you to cut down into small pieces, it means that you are providing a perfect venue for tenderizing, either wholly or relatively depending on how large or small the pieces. You are required to prepare the ingredients by removing the unnecessary as per the directions to achieve the best results. All food requirements in this book can join the wok after proper cutting, dicing and stripping.

In all recipes, one of the instructions is to burn the oil until it is smoking hot. At such high temperatures, the fat begins to break down. So, your oil selection should be able withstand high amounts of heat. Vegetable oil is an excellent choice, but peanut is the best since it has a high smoking point, not to mention the flavor.

There will be liquids that you will need to be aware of in the course of reading the book. Soy sauce, hot and sweet chili, sherry wine (fortified type) and various kinds of broths. For the soups, you should know how to prepare them. Most of the sauces should be thick, so the ingredients you choose are a significant factor to the overall effect on flavor.

Selecting The Equipment

You will need the following when preparing stir-fries:

- A wok, large skillet or a large non-stick frying pan. If you own them all, that's great.
- Spatula or chopsticks
- Bowls of different sizes
- Serving platters
- Colander – a bowl-shaped strainer
- Paper/kitchen towels
- Chopping board and knives
- Spoons and forks
- Blender/food processor

You can add other items if required while stir-frying. I have specified other things you might need in individual recipes apart from the usual ones. You can mark them as you continue reading.

Chapter 1: Pork Stir-Fry Recipes

Most of us have consumed pork for a long time. However, stir-frying it changes every other view you might have about this type of meat. Check this collection of recipes to make the best out of pork.

1. Ginger-Lemon Pork

Cooking time: 30 minutes
Serving: 4

Ingredients

- Pork tenderloin – 1 pound
- Angel hair pasta – 8 ounces
- Vegetable oil – 1
- Cornstarch – 1 tablespoon
- Pepper – 1/8 teaspoon
- Salt – ¼ teaspoon
- Sugar-snap peas – 6 ounces
- Fresh lemon juice – ½ cup
- Sweet red pepper, cut it into ¼-inch broad slices – 1
- Fresh grated ginger – 1 teaspoon
- Bottled chili sauce – 2 tablespoons
- Grated lemon rind – 1 teaspoon

- Chopped scallions – ¼ cup

Directions

1. Start by cooking the angel hair pasta following directions on the package. Drain when ready and rinse with cold water. After rinsing, put it aside and move to the next step. Use a meat board and knife to cut the pork tenderloin into ¼-inch thick slices.
2. With all ingredients measured, mix the pork with cornstarch, vegetable oil, salt, and pepper in a large bowl. Trim the sugar-snap peas and then proceed to heat the oil (1 tablespoon) in a skillet on extreme heat.
3. Put the sliced pork in the skillet and stir-fry for three minutes until it browns. Add the peas and pepper strips. After stir-frying for another three minutes, empty the contents in a large bowl.
4. Back to the skillet, boil sugar and a quarter of the lemon juice for three minutes until they turn caramel (yellow-brown). Add the remaining ¼ cup of lemon juice, chili sauce, ground lemon rind, and ginger.
5. Stir a bit and then add the vegetables, pork, and pasta. Cook by stirring so that everything heats through. Switch off the heat and sprinkle with scallions after serving.

2. Spicy Black Bean Sauce Pork

Cooking time: 20 minutes
Serving: 2

Ingredients

- Pork tenderloin, trim and cut into strips – 300 grams
- Frying oil
- Corn flour – 1 tablespoon
- Sliced green pepper – 1
- Sliced onion – 1
- Shredded Ginger– 1
- Chili flakes – 1 pinch
- Crushed Sichuan peppercorns – 1 tablespoon
- Black bean sauce – 6 tablespoons
- Cooked egg noodles. Heat before serving.

Directions

1. Here, you need to season the pork first by tossing with corn flour. After that, take a wok and heat two tablespoons of oil until hot. Put the coated pork in the wok and stir-fry until golden.
2. Put the pork in a bowl and proceed to add one more tablespoon of oil in the wok followed by the cut onions and pepper.
3. Stir-fry to soften the pepper and onions. Add ginger, chili, and peppercorns and cook them for one minute.
4. Put the black bean sauce and add water (100ml). Reduce the heat to medium for the food to simmer.
5. Put the pork back to the wok and toss it until it is heated through. Switch off the heat and serve together with noodles.

3. Sticky Pork And Mange Tout

Cooking time: 20 minutes
Serving: 2

Ingredients

- Thin pork slices, cut into strips – 300 grams
- Corn flour – 1 tablespoon
- Egg noodles, dried – 100 grams
- Frying oil
- Mangetout, halved – 100 grams
- Honey – 1 tablespoon
- Lemon, juiced – 1

- Chili sauce – 2 tablespoons
- Soy sauce – 2 tablespoons

Directions

1. Cook the noodles in a pot following the package instructions and make sure they are well drained. As

the noodles cook, prepare the pork by tossing it with corn flour.
2. When the pork is ready, take a wok or a big non-stick fry pan and heat one tablespoon of oil. Put the meat in the wok or pan and stir-fry it for two minutes before you scoop it out and set aside.
3. Add mangetout and some of the spring onions and then toss for some minutes. Put the pork back and add lemon, soy, honey, and chili.
4. Splash in some water and let the food bubble for at least 3 minutes or until you get a sauce.
5. Finish up by tossing in the noodles until they are heated through. Sprinkle the remaining spring onions before serving.

4. Pork With Lo Mein Noodles And Vegetables

Cooking time: 40 minutes
Serving 4

Ingredients

- Fresh Lo Mein noodles – 450 grams
- Kosher salt
- Boneless country-style pork ribs – 450 grams
- Sugar – 3 tablespoons
- Baking soda – 1 teaspoon
- Oyster sauce – 3 tablespoons
- Soy sauce – 3 tablespoons
- Balsamic vinegar – 2 tablespoons
- Dry sherry – 2 tablespoons
- Toasted sesame oil – 1 tablespoon
- Fish sauce – 1 tablespoon
- Neutral oil such as canola or peanut – 3 tablespoons, divided

- Ginger knob, minced – 1
- Cornstarch – 1 tablespoon
- Minced medium garlic cloves – 3
- Shredded and cored purple cabbage – 1 ½ cups (150 grams)
- Scallions, green parts thinly sliced, cut the white parts into 1-inch pieces – 4
- Cored Napa cabbage, or shredded Chinese broccoli – 1 ½ cups (150 grams)
- Carrots, cut into long thin strips – 1 cup (75 grams)

Directions

1. Cook the noodles using salted boiling water according to the instructions. Make sure they are firm to be eaten and separated before draining and setting aside. Trim the pork to get rid of excess fat before you cut it into 2 inches long and a ¼-inch wide slices.
2. Put baking soda in a bowl and stir after adding half a cup of cold water. Put the pork in the bowl with the baking soda mixture and stir to get a full coating. In that state, let them stay for the next 15 minutes.
3. As you wait, take another medium bowl and whisk together the following: sugar, oyster sauce, soy sauce, sesame oil, vinegar, fish sauce, wine, and cornstarch. When the sugar is fully dissolved, set it aside.
4. Drain the pork and rinse it with water (cold) before using paper towels to pat dry. Rinse and dry the

bowl that had pork and add the meat back. Add two tablespoons of the sauce you prepared in step 5 and mix thoroughly.
5. Take a wok or a skillet and heat a tablespoon of neutral oil on medium heat until it shimmers. Proceed by adding garlic, ginger and the white scallion parts and stir-fry them for 30 seconds.
6. Switch the heat to high and then add the cabbage, carrots and Napa cabbage or broccoli depending on what you chose. Stir and toss until the contents you added in step 10 are cooked through. Are they ready? Transfer everything to a plate.
7. Clean the skillet or wok by wiping out. After cleaning, put one tablespoon of neutral oil and heat until it's smoking hot. Add noodles to the wok and toss as you stir until they become hot.
8. Now, add the earlier made pork together with the rest of the sauce, veggies, and noodles. Stir-fry everything so that the meat can mix with the added ingredients.
9. Put the meat and lo Mein on a platter and sprinkle the green scallion parts. If you still got the sesame seeds, sprinkle along. Serve right away.

5. Spicy Ground Pork With Cucumbers

Cooking time: 1 hour
Serving: 2-4

Ingredients

Marinated pork ingredients

- Ground pork – 225 grams
- Shaoxing wine (traditional Chinese wine made from rice) – 1 teaspoon
- Soy sauce – 1 teaspoon
- Asian fish sauce – 1 teaspoon
- Vegetable oil – 1 teaspoon
- Cornstarch – ½ teaspoon

Sauce and stir-fry ingredients

- Soy sauce – 1 teaspoon

- Cornstarch – ½ teaspoon
- Toasted sesame oil – 1 teaspoon
- Chili flakes for the taste – 1 teaspoon
- Vegetable oil – 1 teaspoon and 1 tablespoon, divided
- Peeled and sliced garlic head – ½ head
- Cooked white rice and ready to serve

Other ingredients

- Large cucumbers - 2 pounds or 3
- Kosher salt – 1 ½ teaspoons

Directions

1. First, partially peel the cucumbers vertically in an alternating peeling and un-peeling manner. Extract the seeds before you cut them into ¼-inch slices. Put the cucumbers in a bowl and add some salt. Toss and mix so that the cucumbers can release some water. It will take you a minute or so. Let it stay in that condition for 30 minutes.
2. As you wait for the cucumbers, it is now time to marinate the pork. Take a small bowl and put the ground pork. Follow by adding the following to the meat: soy sauce, oil, Shaoxing wine, cornstarch and fish sauce.
3. Mix everything thoroughly and refrigerate for 30 minutes or so. Do you have time? Let it stay

overnight. A good idea is to prepare it before practicing this recipe.
4. In the meantime, take a small bowl and add the following: water, sesame oil, soy sauce and cornstarch. Mix them thoroughly before setting the bowl aside. Go back to the cucumbers and drain them before rinsing with running cold water. Drain them again and pat dry using paper towels.
5. With all the above ready, take a wok and heat a teaspoon of vegetable oil over high heat until it's hot. Put the marinated pork and spread it out using a spatula to get a thin layer in the wok. Let it cook for 30 seconds and don't disturb it as you wait.
6. After 30 seconds are over, split the pork into smaller pieces using the spatula. Add the chili flakes and stir-fry until the pork turns golden brown. Put the contents in a bowl and set them aside.
7. Clean the wok by wiping. After that, add a teaspoon of vegetable oil and overheat. When the oil is hot, add garlic and stir for the next 10 seconds before adding the cucumbers. Continue to mix for at least two minutes.
8. Put the pork back and keep stirring. When the pork has mixed well with the already put ingredients, take the sauce and mix a little with a spoon before pouring it to the wok.
9. After the pour, cook and stir until the cucumbers become glossy. It will take you about 30 seconds. Switch off the heat and empty the wok to a plate. Serve the stir-fry immediately with the cooked rice.

6. Sweet And Sour Pork

Note: Water-velveting makes the meat strips tender. Prepare this recipe if you have time, probably on the weekend if not during the night.

Cooking time: 1hour
Serving: 2

Ingredients

Pork **Ingredients**

- Cornstarch – 2 teaspoons
- A lightly beaten egg white – 1 tablespoon
- Chinese rice wine (Shaoxing wine) – 2 teaspoons
- Pork loin, 1/8-inch slices – ½ pound (225 grams)

- Kosher salt – ¼ teaspoon
- Vegetable or canola oil – 1 teaspoon
- Water – 6 cups

Stir-fry ingredients

- Tomato paste – 1 teaspoon
- Canned pineapple chunks – ½ cup
- Canned pineapple juice – 4 tablespoons
- Soy sauce – 2 teaspoons

- Rice vinegar – 2 tablespoons
- Cornstarch – 1 teaspoon
- Sesame oil – ½ teaspoon
- Vegetable or canola oil – 1 tablespoon
- Red bell pepper, seed and stem it before slicing into ½-inch thick lengthwise slices – ½
- Green bell pepper prepared the same way as the red one – ½
- Small white onion, cut into ½-inch thick slices – ½
- Cooked white rice

Directions

Preparing the pork

1. Take a small bowl and thoroughly mix the cornstarch, egg white, rice wine, and salt. Get another bowl and put the pork in. Pour the mixture you prepared in step 1 over the meat and toss it for

the best coating results. Let it refrigerate for about 30 minutes.
2. After the ½ hour wait, put water in a wok and boil it using high heat. At boiling point, add oil. Add the coated pork in the wok and stir using chopsticks (a strainer comes in handy too), to separate the pieces. Continue cooking for the next 40 seconds, until the pork turns opaque or nearly cooked through.
3. Drain the contents using a bowl-shaped strainer and shake after each fetch to make sure most of the water gets out. When the wok is empty, wipe and dry it thoroughly.

Preparing the stir-fry

1. Take a small bowl and mix the following: Tomato paste, pineapple juice, soy sauce, rice vinegar, cornstarch and sesame oil. Go back to the wok and heat vegetable or canola oil until it's smoking hot. Add both green and red bell peppers, then stir-fry for the next 30 seconds.
2. Add the pork and keep stir-frying until you see some brown spots which will take at least 2 minutes. Get a spatula and move the pork and veggies to the sides of the wok. Add sauce at the center spot you made after moving the meat and vegetables.
3. Let the sauce boil as you slightly stir then start tossing the pork and vegetables for the sauce to coat everything. After an even coat, stop heating

and toss in the pineapple chunks. Serve the stir-fried food immediately with the cooked rice.

7. Pork With Kale And Spring Onions

Here is a great supper option if you want to have a taste of some sweet pork with chili. Ginger and mirin (Japanese rice wine) takes this recipe to another level. You can choose to serve with rice or noodles.

Cooking time: 20 minutes
Serving: 4

Ingredients

- Rice wine vinegar – 1 tablespoon
- Soy sauce – 1 tablespoon
- Mirin – 2 tablespoons
- Trimmed pork tenderloin, cut into strips – 1 pound
- Groundnut oil
- Seeded and finely chopped red chili – 1
- Grated ginger – thumb size
- Crushed garlic clove – 1
- Carrots, peeled and thinly sliced – 2

- Kales, wash and chop them – 200 grams
- Diced spring onions – 3

Directions

1. Start by taking a bowl and mix the soy, mirin and rice wine vinegar. After mixing, take a wok and strongly heat a tablespoon of oil.
2. As the wok heats, take the marinade (mixture in step 1) and dip pork in it. Shake off the excess as you remove, and put the meat in a bowl. Follow by frying in batches until you see a golden color.
3. When golden, take the meat out of the wok and wipe it clean. Heat another tablespoon of oil until it's hot. Follow by frying the garlic, chili, and ginger until the smell reaches you.
4. At fragrance, add carrots then stir-fry for two minutes. Add the onions, kales, marinade and the pork, in that order.
5. Let it cook for 7-8 minutes so that the pork cooks through. When the meat is ready, serve with rice or noodles.

8. Caramelized Pork – Vietnamese

If you cook ordinary or jasmine rice, here is a quick recipe to serve with it.

Cooking time: 35 minutes
Serving: 4

Ingredients

- White sugar – 1 cup
- Vegetable oil – 1 tablespoon
- Pork spare ribs, sliced into 1-inch pieces – 2 pounds
- Chopped green chili pepper – 1
- Green onions, sliced into 2-inch lengths – 2
- Ground black pepper – 1 teaspoon
- Finely chopped shallots (bulb onions) – 2
- Minced garlic cloves – 2
- Salt
- Thinly sliced green onion, separated into rings – 1 tablespoon
- Sesame oil – 1 teaspoon

Directions

1. Strongly heat the wok or a heavy skillet. When it's smoking hot, add oil in a drizzling manner. After the oil, pour sugar on it. Proceed to continuously stir the mixture until the sugar dissolves and turns to light brown.

2. What you just did is caramelizing the sugar (turning into a caramel color). Now, put the pork, some of the green onions, chili and black pepper, shallots, garlic cloves, and salt.
3. Toss the meat together with the added ingredients until the pork turns golden brown. Take sesame oil and drizzle it over the pork and veggies. Turn the heat to low so that the food can simmer.
4. When the juices are almost absorbed, put the heat back to high and stir the food until the sauce thickens and coats the pork. It should take you 5 minutes.
5. Use a tablespoon to sprinkle the remaining green onions over the pork and vegetables before serving.

9. Spicy Pork

This recipe is way too spicy so make sure you have lots of white rice to cover for that.

Cooking time: 1 hour
Serving: 4

Ingredients

- Cornstarch – 1 tablespoon and 1 teaspoon, separate
- Soy sauce – 2 tablespoons and 1 tablespoon, separate
- Cubed pork tenderloin – 1 pound
- Squeezed lime – 1
- Rice vinegar – 2 tablespoons
- Dark sesame oil – 3 tablespoons
- Fresh and minced ginger root – 3 teaspoons
- Peanut oil – 1 tablespoon
- Carrots, cut into long thin strips – ½ cup
- Chopped green chili peppers – 2

- Sugar snap peas, cut into long strips – ½ cup
- Green onions, chopped – ¼ cup
- Chili oil – 2 teaspoons
- Finely chopped peanuts – ¼ cup

Directions

1. Get a medium bowl and put the following in it: soy sauce (two tablespoons) cornstarch (one tablespoon) and water. Mix them thoroughly to get a smooth texture. Stir the pork cubes in the mixture you just prepared. Cover the bowl and refrigerate the marinated pork for at least 30 minutes.
2. Meanwhile, take a small bowl and mix lime, soy sauce (1 tablespoon) cornstarch (1 teaspoon) and sesame oil. Mix them before setting them aside for later use. After 30 minutes in the refrigerator, remove the pork.
3. Turn on the heat, place a wok or large skillet with peanut oil in it until it becomes hot. Stir in the ginger, chili pepper, and salt for a minute.
4. Put the marinated pork in the wok together with marinade and sugar snap peas. Stir-fry for the next 6-8 minutes for the pork to tenderize.
5. When the meat is tenderized, put the lime mixture. Lower the heat to medium for the sauce to simmer and thicken. It should take you another 6-8 minutes. Switch off the heat and stir in chili oil, peanuts, and green onions before serving.

10. Pork And Pepper

You can substitute the pork with beef or chicken if pork is not a favorite when combined with pepper. You can also prepare the marinade or choose not to. In short, you can bend the rules here.

Cooking time: 1 hour 10 minutes
Serving: 4

Ingredients

Marinade ingredients

- Garlic, minced – 2 tablespoons
- Rice wine vinegar – ¼ cup
- Olive oil – 5 tablespoons
- Brown sugar – 1 tablespoon
- Salt and pepper

Stir-fry ingredients

- Boneless pork meat, cut into small bite-size pieces – 4 pounds

- Fresh ginger root, finely chopped – 3 tablespoons
- Vegetable oil – 5 tablespoons
- Hot chili paste – 1 tablespoon
- Green, red, and yellow bell peppers, cut into strips – 1 each
- Teriyaki sauce (homemade for taste preference) – 5 tablespoons
- Fresh mint, chopped – 2 tablespoons
- Briefly cooked splintered almonds – ¼ cup
- Salt and pepper

Directions

1. Get a large bowl and mix the following: garlic, rice wine vinegar, olive oil, brown sugar, salt, and pepper. When the mixture is ready, stir the pork in and leave it for 30 minutes, at room temperature. After the ½ hour wait, heat a wok or a large frying pan using medium heat. Do not add oil.
2. When heated, put the almonds in the dry wok and toast to get a golden-brown color and a sweet aroma. After cooking, place them on a platter or bowl and set them aside.
3. Back in the wok, heat the vegetable oil over medium to high heat. Put the marinated pork, chili paste, and ginger and stir as the pork fries. The rest of the marinade is not useful after this.
4. Put the teriyaki sauce in the wok or pan and increase the heat. With the heat at high level, stir and cook until the pork goes white.

5. Now, it is time to stir the peppers in as you continue to stir until almost all liquid is gone. After, add the almond slivers you toasted together with mint in the frying food. Switch off the heat when the food is ready and serve.

11. Pork, Ginger, And Apple With Hoisin Sauce

Cooking time: 40 minutes
Serving: 3

Ingredients

- Brown sugar – 2 tablespoons
- Hoisin sauce – 2 tablespoons
- Soy sauce – 6 tablespoons
- Pork loin, cut into strips – 1 pound
- Applesauce – ½ cup
- Cornstarch – 1 ½ tablespoons
- Sesame oil – ½ teaspoon
- Peanut oil – 2 tablespoons
- Broccoli florets – 3 cups
- Fresh ginger root, chopped – 1 tablespoon

Directions

1. In a small bowl, put brown sugar, hoisin sauce, applesauce and soy sauce and whisk thoroughly to mix. Set the bowl aside once the mixture is even.
2. In another bowl, mix pork with cornstarch. Make sure the meat gets an even coat before setting it aside too. Take a wok or a large skillet and put sesame and peanut oils. Use medium to high heat for the temperature.
3. Put the pork in three batches in the heated oil. Now, cook until the pink color in the middle of meat pieces disappears. One batch should take you 2-3 minutes before putting the next.
4. After a nearly cooked gesture, put the pork in a plate aligned with paper towels to drain the oil. Back to the wok/skillet, without wiping, put ginger and stir for the next 30 seconds.
5. After stirring, add broccoli and stir until it's tender. Return the meat in the wok and pour the sauce mixture. Toss everything to get a good coating on the meat and broccoli. Is it ready? Serve while it's still hot.

Chapter 2: Poultry Stir-Fry Recipes

Most, if not all of the recipes in this section are perfect for a busy week. Tossing chicken for your family twice per week gets the meal ready before you even know it. Most of the time, you will be using chicken breasts or thighs. Make sure your pieces are uniform when cutting and marinate when necessary. Also let the food cook before heading to the dining table for health reasons of course. Raw or undercooked meat can bring all the unwanted complications.

12. Szechuan/Sichuan Chicken

We start with a chicken stir-fry that is great for a midweek meal. The calories are also low if you like it that way.

Cooking time: 20 minutes
Serving: 2

Ingredients

- Frying oil – 2 tablespoons
- Trimmed green beans – 150 grams
- Thigh fillets from chicken, skinless and cut into chunks – 4 pieces
- Crushed Szechuan peppercorns – ¼ teaspoon
- Crushed garlic cloves – 2
- Dried chili flakes – 1 pinch
- Soy sauce – 1 tablespoon
- Grated ginger – 3cm chunk
- Honey – 2 teaspoons
- Sesame oil – ½ teaspoon

- Chinese rice wine (Shaoxing) – 1 tablespoon
- Rice or noodles, cooked to serve

Directions

1. Get a frying pan and put some salted water. Let the water boil before putting the beans. Let them cook for a minute before draining and setting them aside.
2. After the beans are ready, get a wok and heat strongly before adding frying oil.
3. Add the chicken pieces together with a pinch of salt (measure as preferred) and stir-fry for around 8 minutes until they turn golden and almost cooked.
4. Put the Szechuan peppercorns, green beans, and chili flakes. Let them cook together with the meat pieces for some minutes before adding ginger and garlic.
5. Continue cooking and stirring for 2 minutes. Add the remaining ingredients and toss to get a nice mixture. When ready, serve the chicken with whatever you have (noodles or rice).

13. Ginger Chicken

This recipe is also low in calories and simple to stir-fry. You get a packed sense of flavor in not more than 20 minutes.

Cooking time: 25 minutes
Serving 2

Ingredients

- Briefly cooked almonds – 30 grams
- Frying oil – 1 tablespoon
- Broccoli, cut into florets – ½ head (small)
- Chicken breasts, cut into small pieces – 2
- Thinly sliced or grated carrot – ½ teaspoon
- Baby corn – 100 grams
- Ginger, thumb-size, cut into small sticks – 2
- Baby Pak choy (Chinese white cabbage), cut into halves - 2
- Red pepper, sliced – ½
- Spring onions, 5cm slices – 2

Sauce ingredients

- Soy sauce – 2 tablespoons
- Cornflour – 1 tablespoon
- Mirin – 1 tablespoon
- Crushed garlic cloves – 2
- Sesame oil – 1 teaspoon
- Dried chili flakes – 1 teaspoon

Directions

1. Heat the frying oil in a large wok. Put almonds and fry for a minute until you see a brown color. After browning, scoop them using a slotted spoon onto a plate.
2. Next, generously season the chicken before putting it in the wok. Fry it for 3-4 minutes until it browns. After the fourth minute, scoop and transfer to a plate.
3. Don't wipe the wok and proceed to put broccoli, carrot and baby corn and cook for the next 4-5 minutes until they all look scorched. Stir in red pepper and ginger and let it fry for 2 minutes.
4. As the food fries, take a small bowl and combine cornflour with 100ml cold water. Mix until it's even. Add mirin, soy, garlic, sesame oil and chili flakes into the corn flour mixture and mix them once more.

5. Back to the wok, put the chicken and almonds followed by the sauce you prepared in steps 6 and 7, spring onions, and baby pak choy.
6. Let it to simmer gently for another 3-4 minutes until the onions and pak choy become tender. Make sure the chicken cooks through as the sauce thickens by stirring. When it is all ready, turn off the heat and serve.

14. Cashew Chicken Ding With Celery, Jicama (Mexican Turnip) And Red Bell Pepper

Cook this one if you have a lovely weekend out with nothing much to do. It will take you some hours before meal time.

Cooking time: 2hours
Serving: 2 to 4

Ingredients

- Chicken breast, ¾-inch dices – ¾ pounds
- Soy sauce – 1 teaspoon
- Vegetable or canola oil – 8 teaspoons, divided
- White pepper powder – ¼ teaspoon
- Shaoxing wine – 1 teaspoon
- Kosher salt – ¼ teaspoon, add more if not enough
- Sugar – ¼ teaspoon
- Cornstarch – ¾ teaspoon

Sauce ingredients

- Soy sauce – 1 teaspoon
- Cornstarch – ½ teaspoon
- Toasted sesame oil – 1 teaspoon
- Water – 1 tablespoon
- Finely minced medium size garlic clove – 1

Stir-fry ingredients

- Button mushrooms or stemmed cremini. Cut into ¾-inch dices – 6 ounces
- Celery, cut into ¾-inch size – ½ cup
- Peeled Jicama (Mexican turnip), cut into ¾-inch dices – 1 cup
- Zucchini (courgette), ¾-inch diced – 1 cup
- Toasted cashew nuts – 1 cup, divided
- Stemmed and seeded red bell pepper, cut into ¾-inch sizes – 1, fit ½ cup
- Cooked white rice, ready to serve

Directions

1. Take a medium bowl and thoroughly mix the following: chicken cubes, two teaspoons of oil, Shaoxing wine, soy sauce, sugar, white pepper, cornstarch and salt. Refrigerate the mixture for at least 30 minutes. If you are looking forward to preparing the next day, have it stay refrigerated overnight.

2. To prepare the sauce, combine the ingredients listed for the sauce part and mix thoroughly. Remove the refrigerated chicken mixture 5 minutes before cooking.
3. In the meantime, get a wok and heat two teaspoons of oil until it's smoking hot. Put the chicken in the wok and make sure the pieces lie on the wok surface with the help of a spatula. Cook without moving the meat for a minute. The chicken should turn brown at the bottom.
4. Now, start to stir until the chicken gets cooked through. That should take you 3-4 minutes. At this point, the meat is ready. Put it in a bowl or plate and set it aside.
5. Without wiping the wok, heat another two teaspoons of oil over high heat until it smokes. Add mushrooms and stir-fry for two minutes. They should release some liquid before seasoning with salt. After seasoning, continue stir-frying until the whole liquid evaporates which should take another 2 minutes or so.
6. When the liquid is gone, put the mushrooms in a bowl and place them aside. With the wok in the same condition, put two more teaspoons of oil and heat high until it smokes. At smoking point, add celery, jicama, and zucchini.
7. Cook and stir for about 3 minutes until the jicama slightly browns. After the jicama browns, add the red bell pepper and salt. Cook for two more minutes until the bell pepper slightly tenders.

8. Now, it's time to put the mushrooms back as you cook and stir for another minute. Return the chicken to the wok and stir properly. When the chicken mixes with wok contents, stir the sauce too using a small spoon and pour it into the wok.
9. Stir and cook the meat together with the sauce for a minute or until the sauce thickens. When thickened, turn off the heat and add toasted cashews (¾ cup) as you stir. Put the wok contents on a serving plate. Drizzle the remaining cashews and serve immediately with rice.

15. General Tso Chicken

You may probably have seen this in your favorite joint displaying all-sweet. You can still make it in your home and still match what the restaurant has to offer.

Cooking time: varies
Serving: 4 to 6

Ingredients

- Vegetable or canola oil – 1 ½ quarts (about 48 ounces)
- White rice, steamed to serve

Marinade ingredients

- Skinless and boneless chicken thighs, cut into ½-inch pieces – 1 pound
- Dark soy sauce – 2 tablespoons

- Egg white – 1
- Vodka, 80-proof – 2 tablespoons
- Shaoxing wine (Chinese rice wine) – 2 tablespoons
- Cornstarch – 3 tablespoons
- Baking soda – ¼ teaspoon

Dry coating ingredients

- Cornstarch – ½ cup
- Flour – ½ cup
- Kosher salt – ½ teaspoon

Sauce ingredients

- Shaoxing wine – 2 tablespoons
- Dark soy sauce – 3 tablespoons
- Distilled white vinegar or Chinese rice vinegar – 2 tablespoons
- Sugar – 4 tablespoons
- Bought or homemade low-sodium chicken stock – 3 tablespoons
- Cornstarch – 1 tablespoon
- Sesame seed oil, roasted – 1 teaspoon
- Vegetable or canola oil – 2 teaspoons
- Fresh and minced ginger, 1-inch piece – 2 teaspoons
- Two medium garlic cloves, minced – 2 teaspoons
- Scallions, one bottom part minced – 2 teaspoons; White pieces only, cut into 1-inch lengths – 6 to 8
- Small and dried chili pepper – 8

Directions

Preparing the marinade

1. Take a large bowl and beat the egg white until it foams lightly. Add wine, soy sauce, and vodka to the bowl and whisk to mix.
2. Pour half of the mixture into a separate bowl and set it aside. To the remaining marinade, add cornstarch and baking soda and whisk.
3. Put chicken in the bowl with cornstarch and make sure they are well coated. You can use fingers to do so. Cover the composition with a plastic wrap and place somewhere, aside.

Preparing the dry coat

1. In another bowl, mix the following: cornstarch, flour, ½ teaspoon of salt and baking powder. Whisk until you get a smooth mixture.
2. Take the marinade you poured into a separate bowl and mix with what you prepared in step 1 until you have a coarse and clumpy result before setting aside.

Preparing the sauce

1. Mix the following in a small bowl: wine, soy sauce, vinegar, sugar, chicken stock cornstarch and sesame seed oil.

2. Use a fork to stir until all cornstarch gets dissolved with no lumps. After mixing, set it aside.

Meal preparation

1. Take a wok or large skillet and put oil, ginger, garlic, red chilies and the minced scallions. Use medium heat at this point. Cook as you stir for about 3 minutes until fragrance. Make sure they don't turn brown.
2. Stir the sauce mixture before adding it to the wok. Make sure everything gets out of the bowl by scrapping the contents sunk at the bottom. Cook and stir for a minute or until the sauce boils and thickens. At this point, add the scallion pieces.
3. Stir a bit for the scallions to mix then stop cooking and transfer the made sauce to a bowl. Don't wipe the wok or skillet. Heat the peanut and oil in the wok. As the oil heats, it's time for the next steps. Taking one piece at a time, remove the chicken from marinade and toss it in the dry coat.
4. To make sure every piece is thoroughly coated, toss the chicken in the dry coat using your hands and make sure you press the mixture onto the chicken for adherence.
5. Still, one piece at a time, take the chicken from the dry coat, shaking the excess, and carefully put them in the wok/skillet. Don't drop meat pieces.
6. After adding all the chicken, cook and use long chopsticks (or whatever you are comfortable stirring

with) to stir after adjusting the temperature to medium (325-375 degrees F).
7. Cook for the next four minutes until the chicken is cooked through and looks crispy. Switch off the heat briefly and transfer the meat to a bowl lined with paper towel for draining purposes.
8. When drained, turn the heat on and return the chicken to the empty wok together with the sauce. Start tossing and use a rubber spatula to fold until the pieces have a thorough coating. Turn off the heat after coating and serve immediately with rice.

16. Sichuan Kung Pao Chicken

For the Kung Pao recipe, the difference between the one you may be aware of and this one is mild so, it's a weeknight dish worth trying.

Cooking time: 15 minutes
Serving: 2

Ingredients

Chicken ingredients

- Small and boneless chicken breasts, ½-inch cubed – 2, 6 ounces each (170 grams)
- Light soy sauce – 2 teaspoons
- Shaoxing wine – 1 teaspoon
- Kosher salt – 1 pinch, preferably large
- Cornstarch – 2 teaspoons

Sauce ingredients

- Chinkiang vinegar (Chinese black rice vinegar) – 2 tablespoons
- Honey – 1 tablespoon
- Light soy sauce – 2 teaspoons
- Shaoxing wine – 1 tablespoon
- Cornstarch – ½ teaspoon
- Low-sodium chicken stock or water (choose between the two)

Stir-fry ingredients

- Stemmed and seeded small red chili peppers, cut using scissors into ½-inch pieces – 6-12
- Vegetable oil – 3 tablespoons
- Stemmed and seeded Sichuan peppercorns – 1 teaspoon
- Peeled and grated ginger or cut into small matchsticks – 1-inch knob
- Medium size garlic cloves, thinly sliced – 4
- Roasted peanuts – ¾ cup (150 grams or 5 ounces)
- Scallions, pale green and white parts, cut into ½-inch pieces – 6

Directions

Chicken preparation

1. In a small bowl, mix chicken with soy sauce, wine, salt, and cornstarch.
2. After an even mixture, add the meat pieces and turn them well until you get an even coat with a thin film of the resulting paste. After a proper coating, set them aside.

Sauce preparation
1. In another small bowl mix the following: cornstarch, vinegar, honey, soy sauce and wine.
2. Use a fork to stir until there are no cornstarch clumps.

Stir-fry preparation

1. Take a large wok/skillet and pour a little oil and don't heat. Instead, rub it in the wok or skillet using a paper towel.
2. Now, it's time to heat until the wok smokes then add the remaining oil which should be followed by the Sichuan peppercorns and chili. Stir-fry to get the fragrance which should take you about 5 minutes. Make sure they do not get burnt.
3. After smelling the aroma, put the chicken immediately and stir-fry until the pink spots disappear. It should take you 45 sec-1 ½ minutes.
4. When the pink disappears, add ginger and garlic and stir-fry for another 10 seconds or until fragrant. Follow by putting the peanuts and scallions and stir for 30 seconds.

5. After stirring the scallions, add the sauce ingredients. Continue stir-frying for a minute or so, until all they get an even coat as the chicken cooks through. If necessary, add a tablespoon of water so that the sauce does not clump. Is it ready? Serve immediately with the prepared rice.

17. Chicken With Oyster Sauce And Mushrooms

With water-velveted chicken, this easy recipe is a tender and silky meat guarantee. Adding dried and fresh mushrooms define the flavor and texture.

Cooking time: 50 minutes
Serving: 2

Ingredients

Velveted chicken ingredients

- Chicken breast, 1/8-inch slices
- Cornstarch – 2 teaspoons
- Egg white – 1 tablespoon
- Kosher salt – ¼ teaspoon
- Rice wine (Chinese) – 2 teaspoons
- Vegetable or canola oil – 1 teaspoon
- Water – 6 cups

Stir-fry and sauce ingredients

- A variety of mixed mushrooms (what you prefer), ¼-inch thick slices – ½ pound
- Sesame oil – 1 teaspoon
- Cornstarch – 1 teaspoon
- Soy sauce – 1 teaspoon
- Oyster sauce – 2 teaspoons
- Vegetable or canola oil – 2 tablespoons, divided
- Medium and finely minced garlic clove – 1
- Wood ear mushrooms (also known as jelly ear), rehydrated for 15 minutes in warm water then drained, half the large pieces – ¼ cup
- Water – 2 tablespoons
- Cooked white rice. Ready to serve

Making it

Preparing velveted chicken

1. Get a small bowl and thoroughly mix the following: cornstarch, egg white, salt and rice wine.
2. Take another bowl and put the chicken meat. Add the mixture made in step 1 and combine by tossing then place the meat in a refrigerator for 30 minutes.
3. After the ½ hour wait, take a wok and heat the water to boil. At boiling point, add oil.
4. Put the refrigerated chicken and cook as you separate the pieces using a spatula or chopsticks for

40 seconds. The chicken should have an outer white color but still raw inside.
5. Drain the chicken using a bowl-shaped strainer to shake it off before setting aside. After emptying the wok, clean it by wiping.

Stir-fry and sauce preparation

1. Take a small bowl and mix the following: sesame oil, cornstarch, soy sauce, garlic, oyster sauce, and water.
2. When the mixture is ready, get a wok and strongly heat a tablespoon of vegetable. When hot, add the mixed mushrooms and season them using salt. Cook by tossing and stirring for about three minutes until the mushrooms release water.
3. After the water release, add the wood ear mushrooms (jelly ear mushrooms). Cook then for about 5 minutes until the mushrooms attain a brown color. Are they browned? Transfer the mushrooms to a plate and wipe the wok.
4. In a clean wok, put the remaining vegetable oil (1 tablespoon) into the wok and heat strongly to smoke. Add chicken and stir-fry for two minutes until it is almost cooked through. When the meat appears ready, put the mushrooms back in the wok and stir so that they mix with the chicken meat.
5. Now, it's time to add the sauce. Stir it before adding to the wok. Toss together with the meat and mushrooms for a minute or so until you get a thick

mixture. When ready, put the cooked stew on a serving plate and serve with the prepared white rice.

18. Honey Nut Chicken

Here is an elegant dish with celery and orange honey sauce for a midweek lunch or dinner.

Cooking time: 20 minutes
Serving: 4

Ingredients

- Boneless chicken breast, cut into strips – 1 ½ pounds
- Chopped celery stalks – 2
- Peanut oil – 2 teaspoons
- Peeled carrots, sliced diagonally – 2
- Orange juice – ¾ cup
- Cornstarch – 1 tablespoon
- Honey – 1 tablespoon
- Light soy sauce – 3 tablespoons
- Cashew peanuts – ¼ cup
- Fresh and minced ginger root – 1 teaspoon
- Minced green onions – ¼ cup

Directions

1. Take a small bowl and thoroughly mix orange juice with cornstarch. Add honey, soy sauce, and ginger. After an even mixture, set it aside.
2. It's time for the wok. Heat a teaspoon of oil over high heat. At smoking point, add celery and carrots and cook as you stir for 3 minutes.
3. Still in the wok, add one more teaspoon of oil followed by an immediate addition of chicken and stir-fry for another 5 minutes.
4. Stir the sauce mixture made in step 1 and add it to the wok. Switch the heat to medium and cook to get a thick result.
5. Top the stew with green onions and cashew peanuts and switch off the heat before serving.

19. Garden Chicken

Another one to serve with rice or salad greens is the garden chicken, but it is somewhat a mean recipe since you can only enjoy it alone. With whole pecans and garden vegetables quickly fried with little oil, you have a mouthwatering method that you can only share by telling the idea.

Cooking time: 35 minutes
Serving: 1

Ingredients

- Boneless chicken breasts, cut into strips – 4 halves
- Extra virgin olive oil (made from raw olive juice) – 1 tablespoon
- Small chopped onion – 1
- Carrots, cut into long strips – 1 cup
- Fresh and sliced mushrooms – 1 cup

- Yellow summer squash (harvested immature), peeled and cut into 1-inch pieces – 2
- Peeled Zucchini squash, 1-inch rounds – 1
- Black pepper, ground and coarse – 1 teaspoon
- Halved pecans – ½ cup

Directions

1. Take a wok/nonstick skillet and coat the bottom part lightly with oil. Using medium heat, heat the wok or skillet and put the chicken strips. Cook and stir the meat until you see a light brown color.
2. After browning, add onions and carrots and continue cooking for 3 minutes. Now, it's time to add zucchini, mushrooms, and squash and keep cooking as you stir until the squash starts to soften.
3. When the squash seems to soften, add the pecans and season the wok contents with a teaspoon of pepper. Toss for 2-3 minutes and then switch off the heat once the food is ready. Serve the chicken with salad greens or rice.

20. Avocado Chicken

When combined with snow peas and chicken, the avocado has an exceptional taste. One thing you need to note though, unripe avocados will serve you best since they don't mush as you cook. Try serving with rice and comment later.

Cooking time: 40 minutes
Serving: 4

Ingredients

- Boneless chicken breasts, cut into bite-size pieces – 4 halves
- Firm but ripe avocados, peeled, seed removed, and cut into large chunks - 2
- Soy sauce – ¼ cup
- Chicken broth – ½ cup
- Minced garlic clove – 1
- Cornstarch – 1 tablespoon
- Vegetable oil – 1 tablespoon

- Cremini mushrooms, stemmed and thinly sliced – 2 cups
- Snow peas (Chinese peas) – 2 cups
- Green onions, cut into 1-inch pieces – 4 bunches

Directions

1. Start by taking a bowl and mix the following: chicken broth, cornstarch, soy sauce, and garlic. Stir until the cornstarch becomes smooth before setting aside. Put oil in a wok or a large skillet and heat using medium-to-high temperature until the oil shimmers.
2. When the oil is shimmering hot, put the chicken pieces in the wok. Start to cook as you stir for about 5 minutes until the pink color disappears.
3. When the meat is no longer pink, remove it from the wok and set it aside in a bowl. While the wok is still hot, put the snow peas and cook for three minutes until they become light green and crisp.
4. Add oil, green onions, and mushrooms. Start tossing for about 5 minutes until the mushrooms become tender, and the juice is almost evaporated but not gone. If there is excess juice after the 5 minutes, pour it off. Once all the liquid is out, add the chicken to the vegetables and switch the heat to medium before stirring briefly.
5. It's time to add the sauce. If it's thick, stir it before adding to the wok. After the sauce, stir in the avocado gently and let it bubble for 3 minutes, or

until the sauce thickens. Stir again to make sure the sauce coats everything before turning of the heat and serving.

21. Orange Chicken

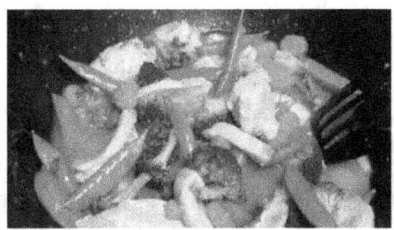

Cooking time: 40 minutes
Serving: 4

Ingredients

- Boneless chicken breasts, thinly sliced – 4 halves
- Orange juice – ½ cup
- Chopped garlic cloves – 3
- Soy sauce – 3 tablespoons
- Ginger, ground – 1 teaspoon
- Grated orange zest (grated orange skin without peeling) – 1 tablespoon
- Vegetable oil – 3 tablespoons
- Crushed red pepper – ½ teaspoon (optional)
- Chicken broth – ½ cup
- Frozen stir-fry vegetables – 16 ounces (1 package)
- Cornstarch – 2 tablespoons
- Sugar snap peas – 1 cup
- Sliced carrot – 1 cup
- Broccoli florets – 1 cup

Directions

1. In a bowl, mix the following thoroughly: soy sauce, orange juice, orange zest, garlic, red pepper flakes, and ginger. After mixing, take a wok or a large skillet and heat oil over medium to high temperature.
2. When hot, put the mixture you prepared in the wok, slowly followed by the meat. Cook and stir for 7-10 minutes until the pink color disappears from the chicken meat and the juices become clear.
3. After the 10th minute, switch the heat to low and take another bowl which you will use to whisk cornstarch and chicken broth together.
4. After making an even mixture, put it in the wok in small amounts and stir after every input until the sauce thickens as preferred.
5. When the sauce thickens, put the frozen vegetables, broccoli, snap peas and carrot in the wok and stir to mix. Continue cooking and stirring until the veggies are somehow soft which should take you another 7-10 minutes. When everything is ready, switch off the heat and serve with hot rice.

22. Duck With Ginger And Greens

If you love duck meat, then this stir-fry recipe will be easy to make not to mention how well it rhymes with ginger and greens.

Cooking time: 15 minutes
Serving: 4

Ingredients

- Skinless duck breasts, cut into thin strips – 2 halves
- Groundnut oil
- Sliced red chili – 1
- Finely chopped ginger – 1 tablespoon
- Sliced Pak choi – 500 grams
- Honey – 1 tablespoon
- Chopped spring onions – 1 cup
- Soy sauce – 1 teaspoon
- Corn flour – 1 teaspoon
- Oyster sauce – 2 tablespoons

Directions

1. Heat the wok strongly and proceed to add two teaspoons of oil. After the oil, slowly dip the duck breasts and stir for 2 minutes. Are two minutes over? Scoop them out to a bowl and set aside.
2. Once the meat is out, add a teaspoon of oil to the wok. Put chili, ginger, pak choi and most of the spring onions. Cook until the choi loses turgidity. After noting pak choi's water release, sprinkle or drizzle the following in the wok: honey, soy and oyster sauces.
3. Once the honey and sauces are in, put the meat back in the wok and let it bubble for a minute. You won't be stirring since you have something to do in the next step.
4. As the meat cooks, quickly take another bowl and mix corn flour with two teaspoons of cold water until you get a smooth texture.
5. Add the mixture prepared above to the meat. Now, begin to stir until the sauce becomes glossy. When the meat and sauce are ready, switch off the heat. Before you serve, sprinkle the remaining spring onions.

Chapter 3: Stir-Fry Beef Recipes

Beef is a typical dish to many but preparing it in the wok needs the right expertise. For most of the recipes that you'll come across in this chapter, you need meat from animals' sides with no bones. Remember to cut it into bite sizes before tenderizing and stirring.

Most of the recipes that I have included take less time amounting to minutes, small pieces will cook through within the stipulated time. If you are still wondering where to get the specified meat, you can go for beef from any part as long as it's boneless and ease your worries in the long run.

23. Crispy Chili Beef

Cooking time: 20-30 minutes
Serving: 2

Ingredients

- Broccolini (tenderstem), cut into small pieces – 150 grams
- Chinese five-spice (a mixture of 5 Chinese-origin spices) – 2 teaspoons
- Corn flour – 2 tablespoons

- Sunflower/groundnut oil
- Sirloin (meat from animal's back), trim off the fat and cut into thin strips – 2 steaks
- Crushed garlic clove – 1
- Grated ginger – 1 chunk
- Dried chili flakes – ½ teaspoon
- Brown sugar – 2 teaspoons
- Soy sauce and brown sugar mixture – combine 2 teaspoons each

- Rice vinegar – 2 teaspoons

Directions

1. Boil some water in a pot and put broccolini when it begins to boil. Let it cook for a minute before draining the water and setting the cut pieces aside.
2. After preparing broccolini, take a small bowl and mix five-spice with corn flour. Once you get an even mixture, toss the steak into the bowl's combination and make sure you achieve a proper coating before taking the wok.
3. In a wok or a heavy non-stick frying pan, heat a small pool of oil over medium to high heat. When the oil is hot, add the steak and fry until it attains a dark golden color.
4. When you finally note the meat's color change, remove it and transfer to a bowl as you drain some of the oil after each scoop. The remaining oil in the wok/pan should be about a teaspoon.
5. Add garlic, chili flakes, and ginger to the oil you saved in the wok. Cook for a minute before putting broccolini. Toss for another minute until the tenderstem is heated through.
6. After the tossing minute, put the steak back and add the rice vinegar and soy sauce. Make sure everything coats before turning off the heat. Serve the beef with rice.

24. Beef And Black Bean

With less than 300 calories and plenty of flavors, this recipe results to healthier food intake as you look forward to ignoring the regular takeaway.

Cooking time: 10 minutes
Serving: 2

Ingredients

- Cube or minute steak, cut into strips – 300 grams
- Grated ginger – 2cm piece
- Finely sliced garlic cloves – 2
- Trimmed and briefly cooked green beans – 2 handfuls
- Black bean sauce (or one with chili) – 4 tablespoons
- Cooking oil
- Cooked brown rice to serve

Directions

1. Take a wok and put a tablespoon of oil. Heat the oil strongly before adding ginger and garlic. Follow by putting beef in the wok and cook until the meat starts to brown.
2. At browning point, add the green beans and stir-fry for a minute. As you stir, add the bean sauce and splash some water. After the water splash, move everything by stirring to get an even coat.
3. Keep stirring as you let the meat cook for 1-2 minutes before removing the wok from heat. At this point, it's now ready to serve with the cooked rice.

25. Beef With Chinese Broccoli

Cooking time: 1 hour
Serving: 2-4

Ingredients

Beef and marinade ingredients

- Beefsteak (from animal's sides), cut into 1/8-inch thick slices – ¾ pounds
- Shaoxing wine – ½ teaspoon
- Soy sauce – ½ teaspoon
- Vegetable/canola oil – 2 teaspoons
- Kosher salt – ½ teaspoon
- Cornstarch – ½ teaspoon
- Sugar – ¼ teaspoon
- Ground white pepper – ¼ teaspoon

Sauce ingredients

- Sesame oil – 1 teaspoon
- Soy sauce – 1 teaspoon
- Oyster sauce – 2 teaspoons
- Cornstarch – 1 teaspoon
- Water – 2 tablespoons

Stir-fry ingredients

- Chinese broccoli, cut into 2-3 pieces diagonally – ½ pound
- Sliced shallots – 2
- Vegetable/canola oil – 2 tablespoons
- Chopped garlic cloves into relatively large pieces – 8

Directions

1. Take a medium bowl and combine all ingredients in the beef marinade section. Mix them thoroughly before setting the bowl aside to let the mixture stand for 30 minutes at room temperature.
2. As you wait, take another bowl and combine the ingredients in the sauce section. Mix them well before setting aside. When the 30-minute period is over, take a wok and fill it halfway with water. Season the water with salt and leave it to boil.
3. At boiling point, add Chinese broccoli and cook for a minute or until you reach a crisp-tender state. After the minute or so, drain the broccoli and set it aside in a bowl or plate. Wipe the wok and then add a

tablespoon of oil. Place it over high heat and let it smoke.
4. At smoking point, add beef and spread it out to an even layer in the wok and using chopsticks or a spatula. Cook without moving the beef for a minute. The beef should be light brown at the bottom before going to the next step. Start stirring and don't stop as you cook for two more minutes until the beef cooks halfway. At this point, transfer the beef to a bowl and set aside.
5. In the empty wok, add a tablespoon of oil and heat vigorously to smoke. At smoking point, put garlic and shallots. Start cooking as you stir continuously for a minute until they soften.
6. Now, it's time to add Chinese broccoli. After the addition, frequently stir for a minute before you season with salt. After seasoning, put the beef back in the wok and toss to get a nice combination.
7. After tossing, get the sauce. Stir it before putting in the wok. Make sure you aim it at the center as you pour.
8. Mix the meat and sauce for coating purposes. Keep cooking as you stir for a minute until the sauce starts to thicken. Upon thickening, immediately transfer the cooked meat to a platter and serve with cooked white rice.

26. Beef With Snap Peas And Oyster Sauce

In this quick stir-fry recipe, you need a steak of beef meat that is flappy (flattened and 'wavy') as the primary dish with snap peas adding more to the taste and appearance.

Cooking time: 30 minutes
Serving: 4

Ingredients

Beef ingredients

- Thinly sliced steak of flap meat – 1 pound
- Sugar – ½ teaspoon
- Kosher salt – ½ teaspoon
- Shaoxing wine – 1 teaspoon
- Dark soy sauce – 1 teaspoon
- Baking soda – 1/8 teaspoon
- Toasted sesame oil (roasted) – ½ teaspoon

- Cornstarch – ½ teaspoon

Stir-fry ingredients

- Shaoxing wine – 2 tablespoon
- Dark soy sauce – 2 tablespoons
- Oyster sauce – ¼ cup
- Low-sodium chicken stock (homemade or from the store) – ¼ cup
- Toasted sesame oil – 1 teaspoon
- Sugar – 2 tablespoons
- Cornstarch – 1 teaspoon
- Trimmed snap peas – 1 pound
- Finely minced medium garlic cloves – 2
- Vegetable or canola oil – 3 tablespoons
- Finely minced fresh ginger – 2 teaspoons
- Finely minced scallion, white and light green parts – 1

Directions

1. In a small bowl, combine everything in the beef ingredients section. Toss the combination to mix and leave it for the next 20 minutes.
2. Meanwhile, in another bowl, stir to combine everything in the stir-fry ingredients section. Set it aside too after a thorough mixing chore.
3. After the mixing task, get a wok and heat a tablespoon of oil over high heat until it smokes.

After smoking the oil, put half of the beef in the wok and spread it to achieve a single layer in the wok.
4. Cook without moving the meat for a minute until the sides attached to the wok have a light brown color. After an underneath browning of the meat, start to toss and stir frequently for another minute to cook it lightly through.
5. At this point, put the beef in a bowl and place it aside. Repeat steps and always remember to add a tablespoon of oil for the remaining meat as you repeat.
6. After the light cooking and setting aside beef preparation, wipe the wok and proceed to heat the remaining tablespoon of oil until it's smoking hot.
7. When the oil smokes, put snap peas in the wok. Cook as you stir and toss until they have charred spots but with a bright green coloring.
8. Follow by adding ginger, garlic, and scallions. Continue cooking as you stir until a sweet aroma reaches you. Return the beef to the wok and toss for a good combination.
9. Next, stirring the sauce briefly and add to the wok. Toss and stir continuously for a minute. The sauce should thicken and coat the beef and veggies evenly. Have you coated the meat and vegetables properly? Turn off the heat and serve immediately.

27. Chinese Pepper Steak

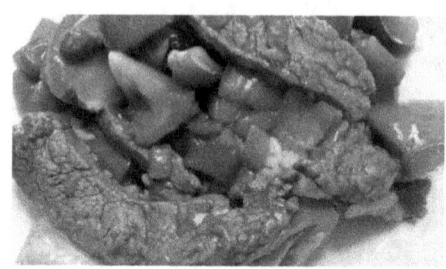

Cooking time: 30 minutes
Serving: 4

Ingredients

- Beef sirloin steak (cut from the abdomen area) – 1 pound
- Soy sauce – ¼ cup
- Cornstarch – 2 tablespoons
- White sugar – 2 tablespoons
- Vegetable oil – 3 tablespoons, divided
- Ground ginger – ½ teaspoon
- Red onion, cut into 1-inch square pieces – 1
- Tomatoes, cut into wedges - 2
- Green bell pepper, cut into 1-inch pieces – 1

Directions

1. First, cut the steak against the grain (against the fiber lining) into ½-inch thick pieces.
2. Next, start preparing the marinade by taking a bowl and thoroughly mixing the following: sugar, soy sauce, ginger, and cornstarch. Make sure all sugar has dissolved, and you have a smooth mixture.
3. Put the beef slices in the marinade and make sure they coat well by stirring. After marinating, it is time to use the wok.
4. In a wok or a large skillet, heat a tablespoon of vegetable oil over medium to high heat. Follow by putting a third of the steak into the oil. Cook by stirring the meat for three minutes, until the beef is all-around brown.
5. In the fourth minute, remove the meat by scooping and set aside. Repeat step 5 for the remaining beef, setting aside each time in the same bowl or plate. Since you are taking a third each time, you will do it twice.
6. While the wok is still hot and unwiped, put all the beef back in. Start stirring and put the onions in the process. Toss the beef and onions for two minutes or so, until the onions start to soften.
7. Now, it's time to add the green pepper and stir. Let it cook as you keep stirring for two minutes. The pepper should turn bright green and start to tender. As the pepper tenderizes, add tomatoes to the mixture. Stir everything and serve when it is ready.

28. Quick Beef Recipe

Cooking time: 25 minutes
Serving: 4

Ingredients

- Beef sirloin, cut into 2-inch strips – 1 pound
- Broccoli florets – ½ cup
- Vegetable oil – 2 tablespoons
- Red bell pepper, cut matchstick-wise – 1
- Chopped green onion – 1
- Thinly sliced carrots – 2
- Minced garlic – 1 teaspoon
- Toasted sesame seeds – 2 tablespoons

- Soy sauce – 2 tablespoons

Directions

1. In a large wok/skillet, heat the vegetable oil using the medium to high heat. With the oil hot, stir in the beef and cook for 3-4 minutes until it attains a brown color.
2. After the browning gesture, scoop the meat out and put it in a bowl. In an empty wok, add broccoli, carrots, bell pepper, garlic and green onions to the wok and aim at the center as you put them. Cook as you stir the veggies for two minutes.
3. When they start to become tender, return the beef and stir together with the vegetables to mix everything. Is the mixture okay? Season the meat using sesame seeds and soy sauce.
4. Now, cook and stir for another 2 minutes until the vegetables seem to tenderize. When the veggies are ready and the beef is cooked through, turn off the heat and serve.

29. Orange Zest Beef (Spicy)

It takes more than an hour to prepare this recipe so, it's a good idea to consider it during the weekend. If you don't like too much fat, it's low in this recipe.

Cooking time: 2 hours
Serving: 4

Ingredients

- Beef tenderloin, ½-inch strips – 1 pound
- Seasoned rice vinegar (sugar and salt added) – ¼ cup
- Orange juice – ¼ cup
- Hot chili paste – 1 tablespoon
- Soy sauce – 2 tablespoons
- Brown sugar – 1 tablespoon
- Garlic cloves, minced – 2
- Cornstarch – 1 teaspoon

- Grated orange zest (orange peeling) – 2 tablespoons
- Cooking spray
- Sliced green onions, separate white and top parts – 1 bunch
- Fresh and ground black pepper – 1 pinch or as preferred
- Salt to taste

Directions

1. In a large bowl, thoroughly mix the following: beef, rice vinegar, orange juice, soy sauce, brown sugar, garlic and hot chili paste. After mixing, cover the bowl and refrigerate for an hour.
2. After an hour's wait, strain the beef using a colander over a clean bowl and let the meat to thoroughly drain for five minutes. Once you're through, put the marinade (mixture prepared in earlier step) aside for the next step.
3. Put cornstarch and water in the marinade. Dissolve the cornstarch by whisking, then set aside when it's ready.
4. Now, it's time to start cooking. Spray a skillet or a non-stick frying pan with cooking spray and heat vigorously.
5. When the skillet or pan is hot, put beef and cook without stirring for one minute. When the minute is over, start to mix and keep going for another minute.

6. Still, as you stir after a minute, put orange zest and the white parts from the green onions. Let them cook for 30 seconds and keep stirring. Follow by putting the green parts of the onions together with marinade.
7. Keep stirring as you cook so that the beef is no longer pink inside and also allow the sauce to thicken. It should take you 2-3 minutes. Season with black pepper and salt to taste before you turn off the heat and serve.

30. Sesame Beef

Another one to serve with rice is round steak that is quickly stir-fried with sesame seeds. You can add sesame oil to the marinade if you like the flavor.

Cooking time: 45 minutes
Serving: 4

Ingredients

- Round steak (from animal's rear leg) – 1 pound
- White sugar – 4 tablespoons
- Soy sauce – 4 tablespoons
- Vegetable oil – 4 tablespoons
- Minced garlic cloves – 2
- Sesame seeds – 2 tablespoons
- Chopped green onions – 2

Making it

1. Take a large bowl and mix the following: sugar, garlic, soy sauce, oil, and onions. Once you get an even combination, set the mixture aside.
2. Next, cut the steak into strips and put them in the bowl with the mixture prepared in the first step.
3. Make sure you immerse the meat pieces well. After marinating, cover the bowl and refrigerate for 30 minutes or overnight if you want to prepare the next day.
4. After refrigeration, start to cook the beef in a wok without any oil for five minutes until it turns brown. It should take you 5 minutes.
5. After the fifth minute, add sesame seeds and cook for another 2 minutes. After two minutes are over, remove the wok from heat and serve.

31. Mongolian Beef And Spring Onions

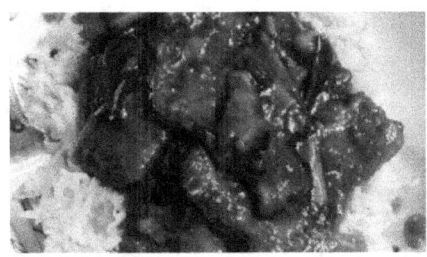

You can serve this soya-based beef with rice noodles or white rice.

Cooking time: 30 minutes
Serving: 4

Ingredients

- Beefsteak (from the sides), sliced to ¼-inch thick pieces against the fiber lining – 1 pound
- Dark brown sugar – 2/3 cup
- Vegetable oil – 2 teaspoons
- Soy sauce – ½ cup
- Finely chopped garlic – 1 tablespoon
- Fresh and grated ginger root – ½ teaspoon
- Water – ½ cup
- Cornstarch – ¼ cup
- Green onions, cut to 2-inch lengths – 2 bunches

Directions

1. Take a saucepan and heat two teaspoons of oil over medium heat. Wait for it to get hot before putting ginger and garlic then stir until fragrant. It should take you 30 seconds.
2. Follow by putting soy sauce, brown sugar, and water to the wok. Switch the heat to high and stir until the sugar dissolves and the sauce boils to slightly thick. It will take you four minutes.
3. Once the sauce seems thick, remove the contents from the wok and set them aside. Switch off the heat before going to the next step.
4. Now that the wok is empty, take a bowl and put beef together with cornstarch. Toss so that the beef can coat with the oil before you let it sit for 10 minutes.
5. After the tenth minute, get ready for the wok. Take it (or a large skillet) and heat vegetable oil to 190 degrees Celsius or until hot.
6. When hot, take the beef, shaking the cornstarch, a few pieces at a time and put it in the hot oil. Briefly stir to cook the meat for two minutes until the edges start to crisp and brown.
7. At this point, the beef is ready for scooping out and putting it onto a plate with paper towels to drain the excess oil. Pour the remaining oil out of the wok/skillet and then proceed to heat it using medium heat with no oil. Wait for it to get hot and then return the beef and stir briefly.
8. Next, take the reserved sauce, stir it briefly and add to the wok followed by the green onions. Let the

mixture boil and cook so that the onions can soften and attain a bright green color. It should take you two minutes before turning off the heat and serving.

32. Black Pepper Beef And Cabbage

Husbands will love this so make sure there is no one in the list of people to feed when cooking this one. You can serve it with hot steamed rice.

Cooking time: 30 minutes
Serving: 4

Ingredients

- Ground beef – ½ pound
- Vegetable oil – 2 tablespoon
- Small cabbage, shredded – ½ head
- Chopped garlic cloves, chopped – 4
- Soy sauce – 2 tablespoons
- Red bell pepper, cut into strips – 1
- Water (preferably cold) – ½ cup
- Cornstarch – 1 teaspoon
- Ground black pepper – 1 teaspoon
- Salt (optional)

Directions

1. Start by putting oil in a wok/skillet and heating it over medium to high heat. Put garlic in the hot oil and cook briefly for 5 seconds before adding the ground beef.
2. Cook and stir until you get an even brown mixture. After browning, scoop the beef out and drain the excess fat before placing it in a bowl and then returning it to the wok.
3. Start to stir and while in the motion, put cabbage and pepper. Keep cooking until the veggies become tender and the beef becomes fully cooked.
4. Now, it's time to put soy sauce to the wok and stir. Leave the wok a bit and quickly take a bowl to mix water with cornstarch. Mix them well before stirring the mixture in the wok.
5. After adding the cornstarch mixture, season the beef with salt and pepper. Keep stirring for the sauce to thicken. After the sauce thickens, remove the wok from heat and serve.

33. Beef With Tangerine Sauce

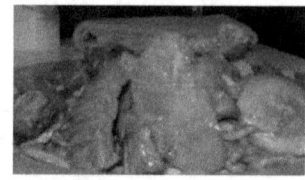

If you do not like the spicy beef, try this one.

Cooking time: 45 minutes
Serving: 4

Ingredients

- Beefsteak (from animal sides), cut diagonally into 2-inch strips – 1 pound
- Dry Chinese noodles – 1 package, 8 ounces
- Sherry (a fortified wine from white grapes) – ¼ cup
- Hoisin sauce – ¼ cup
- Tangerine zest (grate the outer cover while fruit still intact) – 1 teaspoon
- Ground ginger – 1 teaspoon
- Vegetable oil – 4 teaspoons
- Fresh and sliced mushrooms – 1 cup
- Butternut pumpkin, peel, remove the seeds and slice thinly – ½ small head
- Thinly sliced cabbage – 3 cups
- Red onion, large cut into 2-inch strips – 1

- Tangerine, seeded and divided into segments – 1

Directions

1. You should start by preparing the pasta. Fill a pot with water and some salt and bring to boil over high heat. As the water boils, stir the noodles in and let it simmer. Cook as you stir the noodles for 5 minutes so that they can be firm when you bite. When they are ready, rinse and drain before setting them aside.
2. Once the noodles are ready, take a small bowl and whisk the following together: sherry, hoisin sauce, ground pepper and tangerine zest. After whisking, take a wok and heat two teaspoons of vegetable oil over high heat.
3. When the oil is hot, put half of the beef slices and continuously stir for 2-3 minutes until the meat gets a nice brown coat. At this point, remove the beef from the wok using a scoop. Repeat steps for the remaining beef.
4. When the meat is ready, heat the remaining oil (2 teaspoons) and put the onions, mushrooms and butternut squash before stirring them all. Continue stirring for 5-7 minutes until the veggies are crisp but tender and the edges are brown in color.
5. Follow by adding the cabbage. Cook as you stir for another two minutes until they slightly wilt.
6. When the cabbage slightly cooks, switch the heat to medium and stir in the cooked beef, hoisin mixture, and tangerine sections.

7. Once they are all in, cook as you stir for 2-3 minutes until they are all heated through. After the third minute, switch off the heat and immediately serve with the prepared noodles.

Chapter 4: Marine Stir-Fry Recipes

It's time for the wok to do some fishing. In most of the recipes, you can substitute the crustacean, mollusks or fish prescribed with what you like.

34. Shrimp, Eggs And Garlic Chives

If you cannot access the shrimp, replace it with sliced and roasted pork.

Cooking time: 40 minutes
Serving: 2

Ingredients

- Medium shrimp, keep it shelled and remove the dorsal vein – ½ pound

- Vegetable oil – 2 tablespoons and 1 teaspoon, divided
- Baking soda – 1 teaspoon
- Kosher salt – ½ teaspoon, divide equally
- Large eggs – 4
- Ground white pepper – ½ teaspoon, divide equally
- Milk – 1 tablespoon
- Medium garlic cloves, minced – 2
- Garlic chives (Chinese chives), cut into 1-inch length – almost 1 cup (2 ounces)
- Fresh and minced ginger – 1 teaspoon

Directions

1. Start by taking a medium bowl, put some cold water and immerse the shrimp. After that, pour baking soda and stir. Refrigerate the shrimp in the bowl for 30 minutes. After the ½ hour is over, drain the shrimp and rinse with tap water. Follow by drying it using paper towels.
2. When dry, put the shrimp in a small bowl. Add a teaspoon of oil, salt and one part of the white pepper you divided. Mix them well and set aside before going to the next step. Take another bowl, medium size, and whisk the following together: all the eggs, the remaining salt, and white pepper.
3. Once you get an even mixture, start cooking by heating a tablespoon of oil in a wok until it slightly smokes, over high heat. Once the oil is hot, put the shrimp in and stir for one minute.

4. Proceed to add garlic, garlic chives, and ginger. Stir-fry for another minute for the chives to wilt a little bit. The shrimp should also be lightly cooked after the 60 seconds stirring activity. After the minute is over, transfer the contents to a plate and set aside.

5. Put the remaining oil (1 tablespoon) in the wok and heat until it lightly smokes. Put eggs in the wok and switch the heat to medium. Do not stir the egg so that the bottom layer can form. It should take you 30 seconds.

6. Start to scrape the eggs using a spatula from the sides, moving towards the center of the wok. Keep doing it until the eggs are semisolid and halfway cooked.

7. With the eggs almost cooked, add the shrimp and chives to the wok. Gently stir until the eggs are faintly flowing. At this point, turn off the heat, put the prepared food on a platter and serve immediately.

35. Bang Bang Chili Prawn

If you want to cook the bang-bang, first attend to the paste preparation a day before cooking the prawn.

Cooking time: 20 minutes
Serving: 4

Ingredients

Bang bang paste ingredients

- Sriracha sauce (or hot sauce) – 1 tablespoon
- Garlic powder – ½ teaspoon
- Brown sugar – 1 teaspoon
- Sweet chili sauce – 5 tablespoons
- Rice vinegar – ½ teaspoon

- Mayo – ½ cup

Other ingredients

- King prawns (or just prawns) – 175 grams (about 0.4 pounds)
- Stir-fry vegetable mix – 285 grams bag (about 0.7 pounds)
- Frying oil
- Sliced spring onions – 2
- Noodles (choose from Singapore origin if you can get some) – 300 grams (0.75 pounds)

Directions

1. To prepare the bang-bang paste, mix everything in the paste ingredients part well and let it stay overnight. On the next day, take the paste and heat it in a wok or a large non-stick frying pan for 2 minutes.
2. Once it's heated, add the raw king prawns and stir-fry until they turn pink. After obtaining a pink color, remove the prawns and the paste from the wok and proceed to heat a tablespoon of oil without wiping the wok.
3. When the oil is hot, add the vegetable stir-fries and cook as you stir continuously for the next three minutes.
4. After the third minute, add noodles and stir for another two minutes. This allows the noodles to heat through.
5. With the noodles in, put the prawns and paste back in the wok and let the food to simmer without stirring. When ready, remove the wok from heat

and serve before topping every individual plate with the sliced spring onions.

Conclusion

By now, you are familiar with recipes that will arm your kitchen with ingredients and instructions on how to use them as you look forward to achieve the best results of each recipe. Most of them will be switched from one recipe to another so if you note something that you'll be using often, buy it in bulk.

It is actually recommendable that after reading this book, purchase what is common in the methods you pick in large quantities.

Stir-frying cuisine can be hard to grasp especially when searching for the actual ingredients so, you are allowed to substitute when necessary. It will affect the overall texture and taste, but that does not mean you are ruining everything. Regardless of the substitution, all ingredients must be attended to as instructed.

One more thing, you only need one primary cooking instrument, a wok – the definition of stir-frying art. Other named equipment is also valid. So, depending on the quantity, choose something that will fit everything and won't get in the way of stir-frying as you cook.

Having captured what you need for a quick stir-fry recipe, what remains is for you to try and see what awaits you on the other end.

Part 2

Recipe 1: Potato Stir Fry

In this sweet and sour recipe, tender vegetables are simply stir fried with spice and coconut milk and flavored with lime, some exotic. Make sure you don't overcook the potatoes otherwise the potato pieces will disintegrate when they are stir fry into the wok.

Serving Size: 4
Total Prep Time: 30 minutes
List of Ingredients:

- 4 potatoes, cut into small diced
- 2 Tbsp. of vegetable oil
- 1 yellow pepper, diced
- 1 red pepper, diced
- 1 carrot, cut into matchstick strips
- 1 zucchini, cut into matchstick strips
- 2 garlic cloves, crushed
- 1 red chili, sliced
- 1 bunch spring onion, halved lengthways
- 8 Tbsp. of coconut milk
- 1 Tbsp. of lemon grass
- 2 Tbsp. of lime juice
- 1 Tbsp. of fresh coriander, chopped
- 1 lime, finely grated rind

Instructions:

Bring a large saucepan of water to the boiling stage and cook the potatoes for 5 minutes.
Drain thoroughly and set aside.
Heat the vegetable oil into a wok or a large frying pan.
Add the potatoes, the yellow and red peppers, and carrot.
Add the zucchini, garlic, and chili. Stir fry for 2 to 3 minutes.
Stir in the spring onions, coconut milk, lemon grass, and lime juice.
Stir fry the mixture further for another 5 minutes.
Add the lime rind and coriander and stir fry for one more minute.
Transfer into a serving dish and enjoy.

Recipe 2: Turkey With Cranberry Glaze

A traditional Christmas ingredients are given a Chinese twist in this stir fry which contains cranberries, ginger, chestnuts, and soy sauce. It is always very important that your wok is very hot before you add the turkey. Serve it with traditional seasonal vegetables.
Serving Size: 4
Total Prep Time: 20 minutes
List of Ingredients:

- 1 turkey breasts, sliced finely
- 2 Tbsp. of sunflower oil
- 2 Tbsp. of stem ginger, chopped finely
- ½ cup of fresh cranberries
- ¼ cup of canned chestnuts
- 4 Tbsp. of cranberry sauce
- 3 Tbsp. of light soy sauce
- Salt and pepper

Instructions:
Heat the sunflower oil into a wok or a large frying pan.
Add the turkey and stir fry for 5 minutes.
Add the ginger and the cranberries and stir fry for 2 to 3 minutes.
Add the chestnuts, cranberry sauce and soy sauce.
Season to taste and allow to bubble for 2 to 3 minutes.

Transfer to individual plate or a serving dish and serve immediately.

Recipe 3: Beef And Broccoli Stir Fry

This is a great combination of ingredients in terms of color and flavor and so simple to prepare. You can always replace or even add other green vegetables such as green beans, mange-tout and sprinkle some grated carrots in the end to bring some different color.

Serving Size: 4
Total Prep Time: 35 minutes
List of Ingredients:

- 8 oz. of lean steak, trimmed, cut into thin strips
- 2 garlic cloves, crushed
- 1 inch of fresh root ginger, grated
- ½ tsp. of Chinese five spice powder
- 2 Tbsp. of dark soy sauce
- 2 Tbsp. of vegetable oil
- 2 cups of broccoli florets
- 1 Tbsp. light soy sauce
- 2/3 cup of beef broth
- 2 Tbsp. of corn flour
- 4 Tbsp. of water
- Dash of chili oil
- 1 Tbsp. of vegetable oil

Instructions:

Mix the garlic, chili oil, grated ginger, Chinese five spice powder and the dark soy sauce together in a large bowl.

Add the beef strips and toss to coat the strips evenly.

Cover the bowl and leave in the fridge to marinate for several hours.

Heat the vegetable oil into a wok or large frying pan.

Add the broccoli and stir fry over medium heat for 4 to 5 minutes.

Remove from the wok and set aside.

Add the remaining vegetable oil and add the beef with the marinade.

Stir fry for 2 to 3 minutes until the beef is browned and sealed.

Return the broccoli with the soy sauce and the beef broth.

Blend the corn flour with the water to form a smooth paste and stir into the pan.

Bring to the boiling stage. Stir until thickened and clear.

Stir fry for one more minute and serve.

Recipe 4: Tuna & Vegetable Stir Fry

Fresh tuna is a dark, meaty fish and is now widely available at fresh fish counters. It lends itself perfectly to the rich flavors in this recipe. You can replace tuna with swordfish if you prefer. You can serve it with noodles or rice.

Serving Size: 4
Total Prep Time: 20 minutes
List of Ingredients:

- 2 carrots, cut into thin sticks
- 1 onion, chopped
- 1 ¾ cups of baby corn cobs, cut in halves
- 2 Tbsp. of corn oil
- 2 ½ cups of mange-tout
- 1 Tbsp. of palm sugar
- 2 large fresh tuna steak, cut into strips
- 2 Tbsp. of fish sauce
- 1 orange, zest, juice
- 2 Tbsp. of sherry
- 1 tsp. of corn flour

Instructions:
Heat the corn oil into a wok or a frying pan.

Add the onion, carrots, mange-tout, and baby corn cobs.
Stir fry for 5 minutes.
Add the tuna and stir fry for another 2 to 3 minutes.
Mix the fish sauce, palm sugar, orange juice, and zest together.
Add the sherry and the corn flour.
Pour the mixture over the tuna and vegetables.
Stir fry for 2 minutes and until the juice is thickening.
Serve hot immediately.

Recipe 5:Beef And Noodle Stir Fry

A fantastic beef and noodle stir fry with so much flavor that you will adore and so easy to do. Rice stick noodles are wide flat noodles made from rice flour. They must be softened by being soaked in boiling water before use. You can replace the coriander or mint by spinach leaves too.

Serving Size: 4
Total Prep Time: 35 minutes
List of Ingredients:

- 1 cup of rice stick noodle
- 2 tsp. of peanut oil
- 2 cups of beef eye fillet, sliced thinly
- 1 garlic clove, crushed
- 1 Tbsp. of lemon grass, finely chopped
- 2 red chilies, seeded and sliced thinly
- 1/3 cup of lime juice
- 1 Tbsp. of fish sauce
- ½ cup of rocket leaves
- 1 cup of bean sprouts
- ½ cup of fresh coriander, leaves
- ½ cup of fresh mint, leaves
- 3 green onions, sliced thinly
- 1 cucumber, seeded, sliced thinly

Instructions:

Place the noodle into a large bowl and cover with boiling water.

Cover and stand for 5 minutes until tender and drain.

Heat half of the peanuts oil in a wok or a large frying pan.

Next, add the beef and cook until browned. Set aside.

Then, add the remaining oil into the wok.

Add the garlic, lemon grass and chili cook until fragrant.

Return the beef and add the lime juice, fish sauce and stir fry until heated through.

Add the noodles and stir fry until well combined.

Add the coriander, mint, cucumber and green onions.

Stir in and serve immediately.

Recipe 6: Stir Fry Shrimp With Garlic And Coriander

If you like shrimp or seafood this dish is exactly for you. Don't hesitate to add other seafood with it and make it grandiose. Serve it with some nice crusty bread, even do some garlic bread - it will be top.

Serving Size: 4
Total Prep Time: 35 minutes
List of Ingredients:

- 2 packs of noodles
- Thirty shrimps
- 3 garlic cloves, chopped
- 2 Tbsp. of soy sauce
- 6 Tbsp. of lemon juice
- 1 tsp. of curry powder
- Olive oil
- ½ cup of soy bean sprouts
- 3 Tbsp. of coriander, finely chopped

Instructions:
Clean and peel the shrimps, leaving the tail only.
Place all the shrimps in a dish.
Sprinkle the lemon juice.
Sprinkle the curry powder and mix all the shrimps well.
Cover with olive oil and leave in the fridge for 2 hours.

Throw the noodle and cook in a sauce pan with boiling water.
When they separate after 2 minutes remove and drain. Rinse with cold water and set aside.
Sprinkle few drops of the oil marinade and heat using a wok.
Add the garlic and the soy bean sprouts, stir quickly.
Add the shrimps and some of the marinade but not all. Continue to mix everything quickly.
Add the noodles and keep stirring. Stir fry for 3 to 4 minutes.
Add the coriander and stir fry for another 2 to 3 minutes.
Serve immediately.

Recipe 7: Carrots With Pineapple Stir Fry

If you can use fresh pineapple the flavor will be even better and the texture crisper. Do not use canned pineapple in syrup; it will ruin the fresh flavor of this recipe. The freshness of the pineapple and the little sweetness of the carrot will make the perfect combination.

Serving Size: 4
Total Prep Time: 20 minutes
List of Ingredients:

- 1 Tbsp. of sunflower oil
- 1 Tbsp. of olive oil
- 1 onion, finely sliced
- 1-inch piece of ginger root, peeled and grated
- 2 garlic cloves, crushed
- 6 carrots, thinly sliced
- 1 canned of pineapple in natural juice, chopped
- 3 Tbsp. of the pineapple juice, from the can
- 2 Tbsp. of fresh parsley, chopped
- Salt and pepper

Instructions:
Heat the sunflower and olive oil into a wok or a large frying pan.

Add the onion, garlic and ginger, stir fry for 2 to 3 minutes.
Add the carrots and continue to stir fry for another 5 minutes.
Add the pineapple and the juice and season well.
Stir fry further for another 5 to 6 minutes.
Transfer into a serving dish and sprinkle with the parsley.

Recipe 8: Stir Fried Lamb With Orange

Oranges and lamb are a great combination because the citrus flavor offsets the fattier, fuller flavor of the lamb. Serve it with some stir fry vegetables it will go very well or some rice.

Serving Size: 4
Total Prep Time: 35 minutes
List of Ingredients:

- 3 cups of minced lamb
- 1 Tbsp. of vegetable oil
- 2 garlic cloves, crushed
- 1 tsp. of cumin seeds
- 1 tsp. of ground coriander
- 1 red onion, sliced
- 1 orange, juice and zest
- 1 orange, segments
- 2 Tbsp. of soy sauce
- Salt and pepper

Instructions:
Heat the vegetable oil into a wok or a large frying pan.
Add the minced lamb and stir fry for 5 minutes.
Drain any excess fat from the wok.
Add the garlic, cumin seeds, coriander, and red onion.
Stir fry further for another 5 minutes.

Add the orange zest, orange juice, and soy sauce.
Reduce the heat and simmer for 15 minutes stirring occasionally.
Remove the lid and increase the heat.
Add the orange segments and season well.
Stir fry for another 2 to 3 minutes and serve immediately.

Recipe 9: Chicken & Noodle And Oyster Mushroom Stir Fry

A very interesting and easy chicken stir fry recipe with Hokkien or call as well stir fry noodles. They are usually sold in cryovac packages in the refrigerated section in your supermarket. You can always replace the oyster mushrooms with some bottom mushrooms if you prefer.

Serving Size: 4
Total Prep Time: 30 minutes
List of Ingredients:

- 2 cups hokkien noodles
- 2 cups of chicken thigh fillets, chopped coarsely
- 1 garlic clove, crushed
- 1 cup of broccoli florets
- ¾ cup of oyster mushrooms, halved
- 1 red onion, sliced thinly
- 2 Tbsp. of peanuts oil
- ¾ cup of snow peas, halved
- ¼ cup of oyster sauce

Instructions:
Rinse the noodles under hot water and drain.
Transfer the noodle into a bowl and separate then with a fork.

Heat the peanut oil into a wok or a large frying pan.
Add the chicken and cook until browned. Set aside.
Add the garlic, broccoli, mushrooms and onion into the same pan.
Cook until the onion is just softened.
Return the chicken and add the noodles, snow peas and sauce.
Stir fry everything until the vegetable are just tender.
Serve immediately.

Recipe 10:Stir Fry Chili Cucumber

Warm cucumbers are absolutely delicious, especially when combined with the heat of chili and the flavor of ginger. The cucumber is sprinkled with salt and left to stand in order to draw out the excess water, this will prevent a soggy meal. Great idea to serve with any grilled meat.

Serving Size: 4
Total Prep Time: 35 minutes
List of Ingredients:

- 2 medium cucumbers
- 2 Tbsp. of salt
- 1 Tbsp. of vegetable oil
- 2 garlic cloves, crushed
- ½ inch of fresh root ginger, grated
- 2 red chilies, chopped
- 2 spring onions, chopped
- 1 tsp. of yellow bean sauce
- 1 Tbsp. of honey
- ½ cup of water
- 1 tsp. of sesame oil

Instructions:
Peel the cucumber and cut in half lengthwise.

Scrape the seeds from the center with a tsp. and discard.
Cut the cucumber into strips and place on a plate.
Sprinkle with salt over it and set aside for at least 20 minutes.
Rinse well under cold water and use absorbent kitchen paper to dry.
Heat the vegetable oil into a wok or large frying pan until almost smoking.
Lower the heat slightly and add the garlic, ginger, chilies, and spring onions.
Stir fry for at least 30 seconds.
Add the cucumber into the pan with the yellow bean sauce and the honey.
Stir fry further for another 30 seconds and add the water.
Cook over high heat until most of the water has evaporated.
Sprinkle the sesame oil over and serve immediately.

Recipe 11:Chicken Liver Stir Fry

Serve this dish with fried rice or noodles. You can use liver of other animal as well if you prefer. Liver is very low in fat and high in flavor. Normally it requires very little cooking so it's a very good meat to stir fry but for myself I prefer well-cooked liver.
Serving Size: 4
Total Prep Time: 40 minutes
List of Ingredients:

- 1 lb. of chicken liver
- 3 Tbsp. of sesame oil
- 2 oz. split blanched almonds
- 1 garlic clove, peeled
- 2 oz. mange tout, trimmed
- 8-10 Chinese leaves, shredded
- 2 Tbsp. of corn flour
- 1 Tbsp. of cold water
- 2 Tbsp. of soy sauce
- ¼ pint of chicken stock

Instructions:
Warm up the oil in a frying pan or wok.
Reduce the heat and add the almonds and cook until golden brown.
Remove the almonds and put aside.

Add the garlic and cook for 1 to 2 minutes. Remove the garlic.
Add the liver into the flavored frying pan or wok.
Cook until all are nice and brown stirring frequently.
Remove and set aside.
Add the mange tout to the frying pan and cook for one minute.
Add the Chinese leaves and cook further for another minute.
Remove vegetables and set aside.
Mix the corn flour and water together in the pan, then blend the soy sauce and stock.
Return the liver, vegetables, and almonds to it.
Cook for one minute and serve immediately.

Recipe 12:Stir Fry Fish With Ginger And Leek

This delicious and spicy recipe is a really quick fish dish, ideal for midweek family meals or light lunch at the week end. Use any firm white fish which will hold its shape such as cod, monkfish or even haddock. To add more flavor to your dish why not to use a smoked haddock?

Serving Size: 4
Total Prep Time: 20 minutes
List of Ingredients:

- 4 Tbsp. of corn flour
- ½ tsp. of ground ginger
- 4 white fish filets, cut into cubes
- 3 Tbsp. of peanut oil
- 1 inch of fresh ginger root, grated
- 1 leek, thinly sliced
- 1 Tbsp. of white wine vinegar
- 2 Tbsp. of dry sherry
- 3 Tbsp. of soy sauce
- 1 Tbsp. of caster sugar
- 2 Tbsp. of lemon juice

Instructions:
Mix the ground ginger and the corn flour into a small bowl.

Add the fish and coat with the mixture.
Heat the peanut oil into a wok or a large frying pan.
Add the grated ginger and the leek and stir fry for one minute.
Add the fish and stir fry further for another 5 minutes.
Add the white wine vinegar, lemon juice, soy sauce, the dry sherry, and the sugar.
Stir fry for 3 to 4 minutes on low heat or until the fish is well coated with the mixture.
Transfer the fish into a serving dish and enjoy.

Recipe 13: Chicken With Vegetables

Coconut adds a creamy texture and delicious flavor to this stir fry, which is spiked with green chili. You can vary the vegetables in this recipe according to seasonal availability or whatever you have at hand. Try with broccoli or baby sweet cobs; even replace the chicken with pork.

Serving Size: 4
Total Prep Time: 20 minutes
List of Ingredients:

- 3 Tbsp. of sesame oil
- 4 chicken breasts, sliced thinly
- 8 shallots, sliced
- 2 garlic cloves, finely chopped
- 1-inch piece fresh root ginger
- 1 green chili, finely chopped
- 1 red pepper, sliced finely
- 1 green pepper, sliced finely
- 3 zucchinis, thinly sliced
- 2 Tbsp. of ground almonds
- 1 tsp. of ground cinnamon
- 1 Tbsp. of oyster sauce
- ¼ cup creamed coconut, grated
- Salt and pepper

Instructions:
Heat the sesame oil in a large frying pan or wok.
Next, add the chicken and stir fry for about 4 minutes. Season well.
Add the shallots, garlic, ginger and chili and stir fry for about 2 minutes.
Add the red and green peppers and the zucchinis. Stir fry for 1 more minute.
Finally add the ground almonds, cinnamon, oyster sauce, and coconut. Stir fry for 1 minute.
Transfer to a warm serving dish and serve immediately.

Recipe 14: Stir Fried Greens

Eat your greens in this most delicious way – stir fried so that they retain their color, crunch, and flavor. Any variety and amount of vegetables can be used in this recipe, just remember that harder vegetables such as carrots are to be cut finely so they can cook quickly.

Serving Size: 4
Total Prep Time: 15 minutes
List of Ingredients:

- 8 spring onions, sliced
- 2 celery sticks, sliced thinly
- 1 cup of white radish, cut into sticks
- 1 cup of mange tout
- 1 cup of cabbage, shredded
- 1 cup of spinach, chopped
- 2 Tbsp. of vegetable oil
- 1 Tbsp. of sesame oil
- 2 garlic cloves, crushed
- 1 Tbsp. of fish sauce
- 2 Tbsp. of oyster sauce
- 1 tsp. of finely grated ginger root

Instructions:
Heat the vegetable oil and sesame oil into a wok or a large frying pan.

Add the garlic and stir fry for one minute.
Add the spring onions, white radish, and mange tout. Stir fry for 2 minutes.
Add the cabbage and the spinach and stir fry for another 2 minutes.
Add the fish sauce, the oyster sauce, and grated ginger. Stir fry for one minute.
Transfer to a serving dish and serve.

Recipe 15:Five Spiced Pork

Five spices is a ready prepared spicy powder which can easily be found from delicatessens or big supermarkets. It is used in this dish with ginger and peppercorn to make a typical Asian recipe. Serve it with rice or Chinese noodle. You can use chicken instead of pork.

Serving Size: 4
Total Prep Time: 35 minutes
List of Ingredients:

- 1 lb. pork filet, cut into thin strips
- 4 Tbsp. of sesame oil
- 1 inch of fresh ginger, peeled and chopped
- 1 tsp. of peppercorns
- 1 tsp. of five spice powder
- 5 Tbsp. of dry sherry
- ¼ pint of pork broth
- 2 Tbsp. of honey
- 4 spring onions, chopped
- 2 oz. of bamboo shoots, shredded
- 1 mango, peeled and sliced

Instructions:
Warm up the oil in a frying pan or wok.
Add the ginger and stir fry gently for about 30 seconds.

Add the pork and stir fry for 4 to 6 minutes until the meat is well cooked and tender.
Add the peppercorns, the honey, the five spice, and dry sherry.
Add the broth. Mix well and bring to the boiling stage.
Add the spring onions, the bamboo, and mango.
Cook everything quickly and stir all the time for a good 3 minutes.
Serve hot immediately.

Recipe 16:Stir Fried Ginger Chicken

The oranges will add the color and the piquancy to this refreshing stir fry ginger chicken recipe. Make sure that you do not continue cooking the dish once the orange segments have been added otherwise they will break up.

Serving Size: 4
Total Prep Time: 25 minutes
List of Ingredients:

- 2 Tbsp. of sunflower oil
- 1 onion, sliced
- 2 carrots, cut into thin sticks
- 1 garlic clove, crushed
- 2 chicken breasts, cut into strips
- 2 Tbsp. of fresh ginger, grated
- 1 tsp. of ground ginger
- 4 Tbsp. of sweet sherry
- 1 Tbsp. of tomato purée
- 1 Tbsp. of demerara sugar
- 1/3 cup of orange juice
- 1 tsp. of corn flour
- 1 orange, peeled and segmented
- 2 Tbsp. of fresh chives, chopped

Instructions:

Heat the sunflower oil into a wok or a large frying pan.
Add the onion, garlic, and carrots and stir fry over high heat for 3 minutes.
Add the chicken, the grated ginger, and the ground ginger.
Stir fry for 10 minutes or until the chicken is well cooked and browned.
Mix the tomato purée, sherry, sugar, orange juice, and corn flour into a bowl.
Stir the mixture into the pan and heat through until the mixture is bubbling and thickening.
Add the orange segments and carefully toss to mix.
Transfer the stir fried chicken into a serving dish.
Sprinkle with the fresh chives and serve immediately.

Recipe 17:Fruity Duck Stir Fry

The pineapple and plum sauce add a sweetness and fruity flavor to this colorful duck recipe which blends well all together. Try to buy pineapple chunks in natural juice rather than syrup for the fresher flavor. If you can only obtain in syrup rinse it in cold water and drain thoroughly before using.

Serving Size: 4
Total Prep Time: 30 minutes
List of Ingredients:

- 4 duck breasts, skinned and cut into thin sliced
- 1 tsp. of Chinese five-spice powder
- 1 Tbsp. of corn flour
- 1 Tbsp. of chili oil
- 1 cup of baby onions, peeled
- 2 garlic cloves, crushed
- 1 cup of baby corn cobs
- 1 ¼ cups of canned pineapple chunks
- 6 spring onions, sliced
- 1 cup of bean sprouts
- 2 Tbsp. of plum sauce

Instructions:
Mix the five spice powder with the corn flour. Toss the duck in the mixture until well coated.

Heat the oil into a wok or a large frying pan.
Add and stir fry the duck for 10 minutes, until it begin to crisp around the edges.
Remove the duck and set aside.
Add the baby onions and garlic and stir fry for 5 minutes.
Add the baby corn cobs and stir fry for a further 5 minutes.
Add the pineapple, spring onions and bean sprouts and stir fry for 3 to 4 minutes.
Add the plum sauce and return the duck into the pan.
Toss until well mixed.
Serve immediately and enjoy it.

Recipe 18: Stir Fried Cod With Mango

Fish and fruit are a classic combination in a lot of different cuisine over the world, and in this recipe a tropical flavor is added which will gives a great scented taste to this recipes. You can always accompany this dish with rice or even new potatoes.

Serving Size: 4
Total Prep Time: 25 minutes
List of Ingredients:

- 2 carrots, cut into thin strips
- 2 Tbsp. of vegetable oil
- 1 red onion, sliced
- 1 red pepper, deseeded and sliced
- 1 green pepper, deseeded and sliced
- 4 cod filets, cut into small cubes
- 1 ripe mango
- 1 Tbsp. of soy sauce
- 1 ¼ cups of tropical fruit juice
- 1 Tbsp. of lime juice
- 1 Tbsp. of fresh coriander, chopped

Instructions:
Heat the vegetable oil in a wok or a large frying pan. Then add and stir fry the onion, carrots, and the green and red peppers for 5 minutes.

Peel the mango then carefully remove the flesh from the center stone.
Cut the flesh into thin slices.
Add the cod and the mango into the pan.
Cook and stir fry for a further 4 to 5 minutes.
Mix the corn flour and the soy sauce, the fruit juice and the lime juice together.
Pour the mixture into the pan and stir until the mixture bubbles and thicken.
Scatter with the coriander and serve immediately.

Recipe 19:Gingered Broccoli

Ginger and broccoli are a perfect combination of flavors and make exceptionally tasty side dish to accompany any meat or even fish. You can use spinach instead of broccoli too.

Serving Size: 4
Total Prep Time: 20 minutes
List of Ingredients:

- 2-inch pieces fresh root ginger, cut into strips
- 2 Tbsp. of peanut oil
- 1 garlic clove, crushed
- 3 cups of broccoli florets
- 1 leek, sliced
- 5 Tbsp. of water chestnuts, halved
- ½ tsp. of caster sugar
- ½ cup of vegetable broth
- 1 tsp. of dark soy sauce
- 1 tsp. of corn flour
- 2 tsp. of water

Instructions:
Heat the peanut oil into a wok or in a large frying pan.
Add the garlic and ginger. Stir fry for 30 seconds.
Add the broccoli, leeks, and water chestnut. Stir fry further for another 3 to 4 minutes.

Add the caster sugar, vegetable broth, and soy sauce.
Reduce the heat and simmer for 4 to 5 minutes.
Blend the corn flour with the water to form a smooth paste and add to the wok.
Bring to the boil and stir fry for one minute until the sauce thickening.
Transfer the vegetable into a serving dish and enjoy.

Recipe 20: Vegetable Stir Fry

Arrange of delicious flavors, which will capture your taste bud and imagination in this simple vegetable recipe where you can always add whatever vegetables, left in your fridge from the previous day. Basil has a very strong flavor which will be perfect with vegetables.

Serving Size: 4
Total Prep Time: 30 minutes
List of Ingredients:

- 3 Tbsp. of vegetable oil
- 8 baby onions, cut in halved
- 1 eggplant, cut into cubed
- 1 zucchini, sliced
- 1 cup of mushroom, sliced
- 2 garlic cloves, crushed
- 1 can of chopped tomatoes
- 2 Tbsp. of sun dried tomatoes
- 2 Tbsp. of soy sauce
- 1 Tbsp. sesame oil
- 1 Tbsp. of dry sherry
- 2 Tbsp. of fresh basil, cut
- Salt and pepper

Instructions:
Heat the vegetable oil into a wok or a large frying pan.

Add the baby onions and eggplant and stir fry for 5 minutes.
Add the zucchini, mushrooms, garlic, chopped tomatoes, and tomato puree.
Stir fry for another 5 minutes.
Reduce the heat and simmer for 10 minutes until the vegetables are tender.
Add the soy sauce, sesame oil, and the dry sherry. Bring to the boiling stage for one minute.
Season the vegetables well and sprinkle with the basil.
Transfer into a serving dish and serve immediately.

Recipe 21:Green Bean Stir Fry

These beans are simply cooked in a spicy, hot sauce for a tasty and very easy recipe. If you prefer without the chilies just add more garlic, for example. This recipe will go perfectly with any grilled meat or fish. You can try as well with Brussels sprouts instead of green beans.

Serving Size: 4
Total Prep Time: 10 minutes
List of Ingredients:

- 2 cups of thin green beans
- 2 fresh red chilies, sliced
- 2 Tbsp. of peanut oil
- ½ tsp. of ground star anise
- 1 garlic clove, crushed
- 2 Tbsp. of soy sauce
- 2 Tbsp. of honey
- ½ tsp. of sesame oil

Instructions:
Using a sharp knife, cut the green beans in half.
Heat the peanut oil into a wok or large frying pan.
Add the green beans and stir fry for one minute.
Add the red chilies, star anise, and garlic. Stir fry for 30 seconds.

Mix together the soy sauce, honey, and sesame oil in a small bowl.
Stir the sauce mixture into the wok.
Stir fry further for another 2 minutes.
Toss the beans to ensure that they are thoroughly coated in the sauce.
Transfer the green beans into a serving dish.

Recipe 22: Shrimp Stir Fry

A very quick and tasty stir fry using shrimps and cucumber cooked with lemon grass, chili, and ginger. You can serve this recipe with rice and you can use different size prawns.

Serving Size: 4
Total Prep Time: 10 minutes
List of Ingredients:

- ½ cucumber, cut into strips 1 ½ inch
- 2 Tbsp. of sunflower oil
- 6 spring onions, cut into lengthways
- 1 stack of lemon grass, sliced thinly
- 1 garlic clove, chopped
- 1 tsp. chopped fresh red chili
- 1 cup of oyster mushrooms
- 1 tsp. of chopped ginger root
- 4 cups of cooked peeled shrimps
- 2 tsp. of corn flour
- 2 Tbsp. of water
- 1 Tbsp. of dark soy sauce
- ½ tsp. of fish sauce
- 2 Tbsp. of dry sherry

Instructions:
Heat the sunflower oil into a wok or a large frying pan.

Add the spring onions, garlic, lemon grass, chili, ginger, and oyster mushrooms.

Stir fry for 2 minutes.

Add the shrimps and stir fry further for another minute.

Mix together the corn flour, water, soy sauce, and fish sauce until smooth.

Add the corn flour mixture with the sherry into the wok.

Stir until the sauce has thickened.

Serve hot immediately.

Recipe 23:Green Chicken Stir Fry

Tender chicken mixed with a selection of spring greens and flavored with a yellow bean sauce in this crunchy stir fry recipe. Do not add any salted cashew nuts to this dish or it will become too salty. You can replace the greens with other green vegetables such as broccoli or green beans.

Serving Size: 4
Total Prep Time: 20 minutes
List of Ingredients:

- 2 Tbsp. of sunflower oil
- 3 chicken breasts, cut into strips
- 2 garlic cloves, crushed
- 1 green pepper, cut into strips
- 1 ½ cups of mange-tout
- 1 cup of spring onions, shredded
- ½ cup of yellow bean sauce
- 3 Tbsp. of roasted cashew nuts

Instructions:
Heat the sunflower oil into a wok or a large frying pan.
Add the garlic and the chicken.
Stir fry for 5 minutes until the chicken begins to turn golden.
Add the spring onions, green pepper, and mange-tout.

Stir fry further for another 5 minutes until the vegetables are tender.
Add the yellow bean sauce and heat through for about 2 minutes.
Add and scatter the roasted cashew nuts.
Serve the stir fry immediately.

Recipe 24:Sesame Lamb Stir Fry

This is a very simple but delicious recipe, in which lean pieces of lamb are cooked in sugar and soy sauce and then sprinkle with sesame seeds. Be careful not to burn the sugar when heating and coating the meat.
Serving Size: 4
Total Prep Time: 15 minutes
List of Ingredients:

- 1 lb. boneless lean lamb, cut into thin strips
- 2 Tbsp. of peanut oil
- 2 leeks, sliced
- 1 carrot, cut into matchsticks
- 2 garlic cloves, crushed
- ½ cup of lamb broth
- 2 tsp. of brown sugar
- 1 Tbsp. of dark soy sauce
- 4 ½ tsp. of sesame seeds

Instructions:
Heat the peanut oil into a wok or a large frying pan.
Add the lamb and stir fry for 2 to 3 minutes.
Remove the lamb from the wok and set aside.
Add the leeks, carrot and garlic and stir fry for 1 to 2 minutes and keep warm.
Remove the vegetables from the wok and set aside.
Place the lamb and the lamb broth into the wok.

Add the brown sugar and the soy sauce and cook stirring constantly for 2 to 3 minutes.
Sprinkle the sesame seeds over the lamb.
Place the lamb on the top of the warm vegetables.
Serve immediately.

Recipe 25:Pork Caramel And Pineapple

This is my way of doing the pork caramel recipe and I am sure you will enjoy it. Remember, it is important to keep high heat for the water to evaporate quickly, if not your meat will be overcooked. I like to add my pineapple to the meat but instead you can add it to the rice.

Serving Size: 4
Total Prep Time: 40 minutes
List of Ingredients:

- 1 ½ lbs. of pork loin, cut into cubes
- 3 Tbsp. of soy sauce
- ½Tbsp. of all spice
- ½ Tbsp. of ginger
- 1 cups of hot water
- 1 chicken broth, cube
- 2 Tbsp. of olive oil
- 1/3 pineapple chunks or half a tin
- 1 ½ cups of Thai rice
- 4 Tbsp. of caster sugar

Instructions:
Heat the olive oil into a wok or a large frying pan.
Stir fry the pork until they are colored and remove them.

Dissolve the chicken broth with the hot water in a bowl.
Add the soy sauce, ginger, and all spices. Mix well all together. Keep the liquid on the side.
Heat a saucepan with the sugar and few drops of water.
As soon as your caramel is brown, add the liquid to it.
The caramel will harden quickly first but keep mixing it and it will dilute slowly in it.
Once the caramel is dissolved add the pork in the mixture.
Boil over high heat stirring constantly until all the water is evaporated.
You will be left with spicy caramel syrup mixed with your meat.
Add the pineapple chunks with the syrup and mix well.
Accompany with some Thai rice.

Chinese Almond Chicken

Serving: 6 | Prep: 20mins | Cook: 15mins | Ready in:
Ingredients
3 tablespoons soy sauce
3/4 teaspoon salt
1 teaspoon cornstarch
2 teaspoons sherry
3 pounds chicken, skin removed, meat removed from bones and cut into bite sized pieces
1 1/2 cups peanut oil for frying
1 cup blanched almonds
1/3 cup sliced mushrooms
1/2 cup diagonally sliced bamboo shoots
1/2 cup diagonally sliced celery
1/4 cup thinly sliced onion
10 whole water chestnuts, thinly sliced
1/4 cup peanut oil
1/3 cup chicken stock
Direction

In a large bowl, combine sherry, cornstarch, salt and soy sauce. Mix in chicken; refrigerate with a cover.

In a large and deep skillet, heat 1 1/2 cups of peanut oil. Fry in almonds for around 1 minute, till golden. Strain the fried almonds on a paper towel.

Strain all but 3 tablespoons of oil from the skillet. Mix in water chestnuts, onion, celery, bamboo shoots and mushrooms. Cook while stirring the vegetables for 1 minute. Take away from the skillet.

In the skillet, heat 1/4 cup of oil. Cook while stirring in the marinated chicken for 3-5 minutes, till the juices run clear and the meat is not pink in the center anymore. Mix in the reserved soy sauce mixture, chicken stock and the cooked vegetables; simmer for 1-2 minutes, till thickened. Mix in the fried almonds before serving.

Nutrition Information
Calories: 522 calories;
Total Carbohydrate: 6.9
Cholesterol: 100
Protein: 35.8
Total Fat: 38.6
Sodium: 847

Chinese Happy Family

Serving: 4 | Prep: 15mins | Cook: 20mins | Ready in:
Ingredients
3 skinless, boneless chicken breast halves - cut into strips
2 tablespoons olive oil
1 onion, sliced
1 red bell pepper, seeded and cubed
1 yellow bell pepper, seeded and cubed
1 (15 ounce) can baby corn, drained
1 tablespoon white sugar
1 (16 ounce) package frozen stir-fry vegetables

1 cup water
1 tablespoon cornstarch
1 tablespoon soy sauce

Direction

Preheat an indoor grill and use cooking spray to coat. On the grill, place the chicken strips and cook for around 7 minutes. Allow them to slightly cool, then cut into cubes.

In a large skillet, heat the oil over medium heat while waiting for the chicken to cook. In the skillet, place the onion rings and cook for a few minutes. Mix in the stir-fry vegetables, baby corn, and the yellow and red pepper. Raise to medium-high heat; cook and stir for approximately 15 minutes.

Sprinkle in the salt and sugar. Blend in the chicken. Place the cornstarch in water to dissolve and pour into the skillet together with the soy sauce. Cook and stir till the sauce thickens.

Nutrition Information

Calories: 313 calories;

Sodium: 915

Total Carbohydrate: 29.1

Cholesterol: 52

Protein: 25

Total Fat: 9.6

Chow Mein With Chicken And Vegetables

Serving: 4 | Prep: 20mins | Cook: 15mins | Ready in:
Ingredients
2 teaspoons soy sauce
1 teaspoon cornstarch
1/4 teaspoon sesame oil
1/2 pound skinless, boneless chicken breast halves, cut into strips
3/4 cup chicken broth
2 tablespoons oyster sauce
3/4 teaspoon white sugar
1/2 pound chow mein noodles
1 tablespoon vegetable oil
1 teaspoon minced garlic
2 heads bok choy, chopped
1/2 zucchini, diced
10 sugar snap peas
1 carrot, cut into thin strips
2 tablespoons chopped green onion
Direction

In a large mixing bowl, combine sesame oil, cornstarch, and soy sauce until smooth; toss in chicken strips until well coated. Chill, covered, for a minimum of 20 minutes.

In a small mixing bowl, combine chicken broth with sugar and oyster sauce; put to one side.

Bring water in a large pot to a boil. Cook noodles in boiling water for 4 to 5 minutes over medium heat until al dente. Drain and rinse noodles under cold water.

In a large skillet, heat vegetable oil. Cook garlic in heated oil for half a minute; put in marinated chicken. Cook for 5 to 6 minutes, stirring, until no pink remains in the center and is browned. Transfer chicken mixture to a plate. Cook carrot, snap peas, zucchini, and bok choy in the hot skillet, stirring, for about 2 minutes until tender. Place chicken mixture and noodles back into the skillet. Add broth mixture; cook for about 2 minutes, stirring, until heated through. Garnish with green onions before serving.

Nutrition Information

Calories: 526 calories;

Total Carbohydrate: 61.7

Cholesterol: 30

Protein: 29.4

Total Fat: 17.9

Sodium: 992

Chrysanthemum Chicken

Serving: 2-3 servings. | Prep: 15mins | Cook: 10mins | Ready in:

Ingredients

2 teaspoons cornstarch

1-1/2 teaspoons sugar

1/4 teaspoon salt

1/8 teaspoon ground ginger

1/8 teaspoon Chinese five-spice powder, optional

2 boneless skinless chicken breast halves, cut into 1-inch strips

2 tablespoons vegetable oil

1/2 cup chicken broth

2 tablespoons additional chicken broth or sherry

2 tablespoons chopped green onion

1/4 cup chrysanthemum petals

2 cups hot cooked rice

Direction

Take the first five ingredients and mix in a bowl. Add in the chicken and mix to coat. In a frying pan or wok, fry the chicken in oil stir-fry style. Cook until not pink, 5-7 minutes. Pour in broth, green onion, and sherry or additional broth. Heat to a boil; stir constantly and cook until thick, about 2 minutes. Decrease heat, add flower petals and toss together. Best if eaten over rice.

Nutrition Information

Calories: 318 calories

Total Carbohydrate: 34g carbohydrate (3g sugars

Cholesterol: 42mg cholesterol

Protein: 19g protein.

Total Fat: 11g fat (2g saturated fat)

Sodium: 429mg sodium

Fiber: 1g fiber)

Citrus Chicken Stir Fry

Serving: 4 | Prep: 15mins | Cook: 45mins | Ready in:
Ingredients

1 (16 ounce) package dry whole-wheat noodles

1/2 cup chicken stock

1/2 cup orange marmalade

1/3 cup tamari sauce

1 (1 inch) piece ginger root, peeled

ground black pepper to taste

1 lemon, juiced

3 tablespoons peanut oil

2 pounds skinless, boneless chicken breast halves, cut into thin strips

1 (16 ounce) bag frozen stir-fry vegetables, thawed

Direction

Set a large pot with lightly salted water to a rolling boil.

Mix in whole-wheat noodles and return to a boil. Uncover and cook for around 5 to 8 minutes, stirring occasionally, till the pasta has cooked through but is firm to the bite. Drain well and leave aside.

In a pot, combine orange marmalade, chicken stock, ground black pepper, tamari sauce, and whole ginger root piece over medium-high heat.

Boil the sauce and lessen to medium heat. Simmer for 20 minutes till sauce thickens and reduces.

Take sauce away from heat. Blend in lemon juice and leave aside.

In a large skillet, heat peanut oil over medium-high heat.

Cook and stir chicken in hot oil for around 5 to 10 minutes till it is golden, no longer pink in the center, and the juices run clear.

Take chicken out of the skillet and leave aside, leaving oil in the pan.

In the same skillet used for the chicken, cook and stir the stir-fry vegetables for approximately 4 to 5 minutes till vegetables are almost tender.

Take ginger root piece out of the sauce and discard.

Stir sauce and chicken into vegetables and cook for around 1 to 2 minutes till heated through.

Serve over whole-wheat noodles.

Nutrition Information

Calories: 849 calories;

Total Fat: 17.5

Sodium: 1838

Total Carbohydrate: 112.5

Cholesterol: 129

Protein: 67.6

Classic Pad Thai

Serving: 4 | Prep: 15mins | Cook: 15mins | Ready in:
Ingredients

8 ounces medium width rice vermicelli noodles

3 tablespoons vegetable oil

1/4 pound ground chicken

1 teaspoon hot pepper sauce

1 red pepper, thinly sliced

1/2 pound peeled, deveined raw shrimp

3 cloves garlic, minced

2 teaspoons freshly grated gingerroot

1/2 cup vegetable or chicken broth

1/2 cup Heinz Tomato Ketchup

1/4 cup lime juice

3 tablespoons granulated sugar

3 tablespoons fish sauce

1 1/2 cups bean sprouts

3 green onions, thinly sliced

1/4 cup fresh coriander or parsley leaves

chopped peanuts

Direction

Cook noodles in boiling water for 5mins, let it stand; drain well and set aside.

On high heat, heat 1/2 of the oil in a deep pan or wok. Break the chicken in crumbles then pour in hot sauce; cook and stir-fry for 3-5mins until brown. Transfer on a platter then set aside.

Pour the remaining oil in the pan; cook and stir peppers for 3mins then put in shrimp. Cook and stir-fry the shrimp for 2mins. Mix in fish sauce, garlic, sugar, ginger, lime juice, broth, and ketchup; boil. Toss in the reserved meat and noodles until well combined. Heat completely.

Gently toss in sprouts. Add peanuts, coriander, and onions on top.

Nutrition Information

Calories: 553 calories;

Total Fat: 18.2

Sodium: 1298

Total Carbohydrate: 70.2

Cholesterol: 104

Protein: 30.3

Coconut Chicken Stir Fry

Serving: 4 | Prep: 25mins | Cook: 30mins | Ready in:

Ingredients

1/4 cup butter

1 teaspoon cumin seeds

4 large skinless, boneless chicken breast halves, thinly sliced

2 tablespoons vegetable oil

1 large onion, finely chopped

2 large carrots, thinly sliced

4 cloves garlic, diced

1 tablespoon grated ginger

2 teaspoons crushed red pepper flakes

1 teaspoon honey

1 teaspoon ground cumin

1/2 teaspoon ground cinnamon

1/2 teaspoon curry powder, or more to taste

salt and ground black pepper to taste

1 (14 ounce) can coconut milk

Direction

In a large frying pan, melt butter over medium heat.

Cook cumin seeds in butter for about 1 minute while stirring until fragrant.

Stir in chicken; cook while stirring for 5-8 minutes until juices run clear and the center is no longer pink. Drain excess juices, if needed.

Stir in vegetable oil; heat until sizzling.

Stir in black pepper, salt, curry powder, cinnamon, ground cumin, honey, red pepper flakes, ginger, garlic, carrots and onion; cook for 5-8 minutes until the carrots are cooked and the onions are translucent.

Stir in coconut milk; allow to simmer for 10 minutes for the flavors to blend.

Nutrition Information

Calories: 657 calories;

Cholesterol: 160

Protein: 50.6

Total Fat: 45.3

Sodium: 156

Total Carbohydrate: 14.2

Crazy Chicken

Serving: 4 | Prep: 20mins | Cook: 10mins | Ready in:

Ingredients

1 1/2 pounds skinless, boneless chicken breast halves - cubed

1 teaspoon oil for frying

2 tablespoons minced garlic

1 (11 fluid ounce) bottle classic-style stir-fry sauce

Direction

Turn on the oven beforehand to Broil or Grill.

In a skillet, heat oil over medium-high heat. Put in garlic and chicken; sauté for 7-10 minutes until juices run clear. Drain fat from skillet; mix the sauce in.

On a cookie sheet, add chicken mixture and put into the oven to broil until browned or for 10 minutes. Allow to sit for 5 minutes until the sauce is thickened.

Nutrition Information

Calories: 364 calories;

Total Fat: 13.3

Sodium: 809

Total Carbohydrate: 18.9

Cholesterol: 104

Protein: 38.4

Creamy Curried Chicken

Serving: 4 | Prep: 15mins | Cook: 20mins | Ready in:

Ingredients

1 tablespoon all-purpose flour

1 pound skinless, boneless chicken breast, cut into 1-inch cubes

1 tablespoon olive oil

1 large onion, chopped

2 1/2 tablespoons curry powder

1 teaspoon coarse salt

1 teaspoon ground cumin

1/2 teaspoon ground cinnamon

1/2 teaspoon garlic powder

1/2 teaspoon ground black pepper

1/2 teaspoon ground coriander

3/4 cup fat-free chicken broth

1/2 cup plain fat-free Greek yogurt

Direction

In a wide, shallow bowl, put flour. Dredge chicken pieces in to coat thoroughly.

In a large non-stick skillet, heat olive oil over medium heat. Sauté onion in the hot oil for 6-7 minutes or until softened; season with coriander, black pepper, garlic powder, cinnamon, cumin, salt, and curry powder.

Keep cooking for about 1 minute or until the spices are aromatic.

Increase the heat to medium-high. Next, stir the flour-coated chicken pieces into the onion mixture; cook and stir for 3-5 minutes or until the outside of the chicken is browned.

Add the chicken broth into the skillet and simmer. Lower the heat to low and continue to cook for about 8 minutes until the center of the chicken is not pink anymore and the sauce starts to thicken. Add yogurt into the liquid and stir until smooth; keep cooking for 2-3 minutes or until the sauce is hot again.

Nutrition Information

Calories: 203 calories;

Total Fat: 6.6

Sodium: 723

Total Carbohydrate: 9.6

Cholesterol: 59

Protein: 26

Creamy Peanut Stir Fried Chicken

Serving: 4 | Prep: 5mins | Cook: 20mins | Ready in:
Ingredients
1 1/2 cups instant brown rice, uncooked

1/2 cup KRAFT Smooth Peanut Butter
1/2 cup coconut milk
1 tablespoon reduced-sodium soy sauce
1 tablespoon Sriracha sauce (hot chili sauce)
1 clove garlic, minced
1 pound boneless chicken breasts, cut into bite-size pieces
3 cups frozen stir-fry vegetables (broccoli, green beans, mushrooms, red peppers), thawed, drained

Direction

Cook rice following the package's instructions, leave out the salt.

In the meantime, in a saucepan, cook the next 5 ingredients over low heat until fully heated, about 3 minutes, tossing often. Keep warm.

In a big oil-coated frying pan, stir-fry chicken over medium-high heat until turning brown evenly, about 5 minutes. Add 3 tablespoon peanut butter sauce and vegetables, stir-fry until all of the ingredients have been fully heated and the chicken is done, about 5 minutes.

On a dish, spoon in the rice; put the leftover peanut butter sauce and chicken mixture on top.

Nutrition Information

Calories: 546 calories;

Cholesterol: 59

Protein: 35.9

Total Fat: 25.7

Sodium: 524

Total Carbohydrate: 51

Curried Chicken

Serving: 6 | Prep: 10mins | Cook: 1hours15mins | Ready in:

Ingredients

1 whole chicken, cut into 8 pieces and skin removed

salt and ground black pepper to taste

1 tablespoon paprika, or to taste

1 tablespoon butter

1 apple, cored and chopped

1 onion, chopped

1 tablespoon curry powder, or more to taste

1 (10.75 ounce) can cream of mushroom soup

1 cup half-and-half cream

Direction

Set an oven to 350°F (175°C) to preheat.

Put the chicken slices in a single layer in a 9x13-inch baking pan. Use salt, paprika and pepper to season the chicken generously; put aside.

In a skillet, melt the butter on medium heat. Put the onion and apple to the butter, season with the curry powder, cook and mix for 7 to 10 mins until the onion and apple soften. Mix in half-and-half and mushroom soup until well blended; scoop on top of the chicken slices.

Bake in the heated oven for about 75 mins until the juices run clear and no longer pink at the bone. An instant-read thermometer inserted into the thigh's thickest part should register 180°F (82°C).

Nutrition Information

Calories: 389 calories;

Total Carbohydrate: 13.1

Cholesterol: 134

Protein: 39.7

Total Fat: 19.4

Sodium: 471

Curry Chicken And Vegetables

Serving: 4 servings. | Prep: 20mins | Cook: 15mins | Ready in:
Ingredients

1 tablespoon cornstarch

2 teaspoons curry powder

1/8 teaspoon crushed red pepper flakes

1 cup reduced-sodium chicken broth

1 tablespoon reduced-sodium soy sauce

1 pound boneless skinless chicken breasts, cut into cubes

2 teaspoons canola oil, divided

1 cup sliced fresh carrots

2 garlic cloves, minced

3 cups fresh broccoli florets

4 green onions, thinly sliced

Direction

Mix red pepper flakes, curry and cornstarch in a small bowl. Mix in soy sauce and broth till smooth; put aside. Stir-fry chicken in 1 tsp. oil in a big nonstick skillet/wok coated in cooking spray till chicken juices are clear for 5-6 minutes. Remove; keep warm.

Stir-fry garlic and carrots for 1 minute in leftover oil in same pan. Mix in broccoli; cook for 2 minutes. Add onions; cook for 1-2 minutes.

Mix broth mixture; mix into veggies. Boil; mix and cook till thick for 2 minutes. Put chicken in pan; heat through.

Nutrition Information

Calories: 194 calories

Total Carbohydrate: 10g carbohydrate (4g sugars

Cholesterol: 63mg cholesterol

Protein: 26g protein. Diabetic Exchanges: 3 lean meat

Total Fat: 5g fat (1g saturated fat)

Sodium: 389mg sodium

Fiber: 3g fiber)

Curry Pineapple Fried Rice

Serving: 6 | Prep: 15mins | Cook: 30mins | Ready in:
Ingredients

1 1/2 cups uncooked white rice

3 cups water

1 tablespoon curry powder

2 tablespoons Asian fish sauce

2 tablespoons pineapple juice

1 tablespoon vegetable oil

1 pound boneless chicken meat, cubed

1 onion, sliced

1 (20 ounce) can pineapple chunks, drained

Direction

Over high heat, heat water and rice to boil in a saucepan. Decrease the heat to medium-low, cover the pan and let simmer for 20 to 25 minutes until the liquid has been absorbed and the rice is tender. Reserve the cooked rice. In a small bowl, combine together the pineapple juice, fish sauce and curry powder.

Over medium-high heat, heat vegetable oil in a wok or large skillet until oil shimmers. Then add onion and chicken and cook while stirring for about 5 minutes until the onions are translucent and the chicken is no longer pink. Mix in curry mixture, pineapple chunks and cooked rice. Cook while stirring for 5 to 10 minutes until the fried rice becomes hot.

Nutrition Information

Calories: 352 calories;

Total Carbohydrate: 56.9

Cholesterol: 38

Protein: 17

Total Fat: 6.1

Sodium: 409

Dak Galbi (Korean Spicy Chicken Stir Fry)

Serving: 8 | Prep: 20mins | Cook: 30mins | Ready in:
Ingredients
1 tablespoon vegetable oil
2 pounds skinless, boneless chicken breast halves, cut into bite-size pieces, or more as needed
1/4 cup gochujang (Korean hot pepper paste)
2 tablespoons soy sauce
2 tablespoons gochugaru (Korean red pepper flakes)
1 tablespoon mirin (Japanese sweet wine)
1 tablespoon brown sugar
1 tablespoon sesame oil
4 cloves garlic, minced
1/4 teaspoon ground black pepper

1/4 teaspoon ground ginger
2 cups Korean-style glutinous rice cakes (tteok)
1/4 large head cabbage, sliced into strips
1 sweet potato, sliced into rounds
1/2 onion, chopped
3 scallions, sliced into 1-inch pieces, divided
4 leaves perilla leaves, sliced, or to taste
1/2 cup water
1 tablespoon sesame seeds

Direction

Heat the oil in large nonstick saucepan, add the chicken pieces and then cook while stirring for 4 to 7 minutes until almost opaque.

In a bowl, mix ginger, black pepper, garlic, sesame oil, brown sugar, mirin, gochugaru, gochujang, and soy sauce. Transfer to saucepan containing the chicken. Cook while stirring for 3 to 5 minutes until the chicken pieces are well coated and browned.

Mix onion, sweet potato, cabbage, and rice cakes into the skillet containing chicken mixture. Cook for about 10 minutes until the sweet potato changes color. Add perilla leaves and 2 to 2 1/2 scallions and then cook for about 3 minutes until wilted. You can add extra water in case the sauce looks to be drying up. Garnish with sesame seeds and the remaining scallions.

Nutrition Information

Calories: 386 calories;
Total Fat: 7.3
Sodium: 384
Total Carbohydrate: 52.8
Cholesterol: 59

Protein: 25.8

Delicious And Fast Chicken Curry

Serving: 6 | Prep: 15mins | Cook: 35mins | Ready in:
Ingredients
2 tablespoons curry powder
2 teaspoons seasoned salt
2 teaspoons onion powder
3 large skinless, boneless chicken breast, cut into cubes
olive oil, or to taste
1/2 onion, chopped
2 cloves garlic, chopped
1 potato, chopped
20 ounces fresh spinach, torn
5 cups coconut milk
Direction
In the bowl, whisk the onion powder, seasoned salt and curry powder; put in the chicken and coat the chicken in the seasoning mix by tossing.
Heat the olive oil on medium heat in the skillet. Cook and stir the garlic and onion in the hot oil approximately 5 minutes till becoming softened; put in the spinach, potato and chicken and whisk. Add the coconut milk on top of mixture and whisk. Put lid on skillet, simmer the mixture, and cook, mixing once in a while, approximately half an hour till potato softens and chicken is not pink in middle anymore.

Nutrition Information
Calories: 585 calories;
Total Fat: 44.6
Sodium: 482
Total Carbohydrate: 19.1
Cholesterol: 66
Protein: 34.1

Denise's Peanut Chicken

Serving: 6 | Prep: 10mins | Cook: 25mins | Ready in:
Ingredients
1 tablespoon wok oil or peanut oil
1 pound skinless, boneless chicken breast halves - cut into bite-size pieces
1 medium red bell pepper, chopped
1 1/2 cups chicken broth
2 teaspoons soy sauce
1 tablespoon sugar
1 clove garlic, minced
1/4 teaspoon ground cayenne pepper
1 (1 inch) piece fresh ginger root, peeled and chopped
1 tablespoon cornstarch
1 bunch green onions, chopped
1 bunch cilantro, chopped
2 cups chopped dry roasted peanuts
Direction

Heat oil on medium heat in a wok. Put chicken into the wok; cook till juices are clear. Stir in red bell pepper; continue to cook till tender.

Mix cornstarch, ginger, cayenne pepper, garlic, sugar, soy sauce and broth in a bowl; put into the wok. Toss cilantro and green onions into the wok; keep some of each to garnish. Mix and continue to cook till slightly thick for 5 minutes. Mix in peanuts; garnish with reserved cilantro and green onions. Serve.

Nutrition Information

Calories: 437 calories;

Sodium: 155

Total Carbohydrate: 18.8

Cholesterol: 46

Protein: 29.7

Total Fat: 29.1

Drunken Noodles

Serving: 4 | Prep: 10mins | Cook: 15mins | Ready in:
Ingredients

1 (16 ounce) package rice noodles

Sauce:

6 tablespoons oyster sauce

3 tablespoons white sugar

3 tablespoons rice vinegar

3 tablespoons fresh lime juice

1 tablespoon canola oil, or more as needed

1 onion, sliced

1 bulb shallot, chopped

3 cloves garlic, minced, or more to taste

1 pound boneless chicken, thinly sliced

1 large green bell pepper, sliced into strips

1 egg, lightly beaten

2 sprigs fresh basil, leaves removed and torn

Direction

Put rice noodles into a bowl then fill it with hot water. Separate noodles with your hands or a fork. Soak for about 45 minutes until soft.

Mix lime juice, vinegar, white sugar, and oyster sauce in a bowl until the sauce becomes smooth.

In a big skillet or wok, pour enough oil to coat the bottom then put on medium-high heat. Sauté garlic, shallot, and onion for 2-3 minutes until slightly softened and fragrant. Add bell pepper and chicken. Sauté for 5-7 minutes until chicken isn't pink. Place chicken mixture on one side of the wok.

Pour egg in hot wok. Cook for 1-2 minutes until it's a little set. Flip the egg then cook for another 1-2 minutes until set. Break apart egg using a fork then mix in chicken mixture.

Mix sauce and basil in chicken mixture. Drain the noodles then put in the chicken mixture. Sauté for 2-3 minutes until heated through.

Nutrition Information

Calories: 656 calories;

Total Fat: 8.2

Sodium: 446

Total Carbohydrate: 111.7

Cholesterol: 111

Protein: 30.3

Easy Sweet And Sour Chicken

Serving: 4 | Prep: 10mins | Cook: 15mins | Ready in:
Ingredients

3 tablespoons all-purpose flour

1/2 teaspoon garlic powder

1/2 teaspoon salt

1/2 teaspoon ground black pepper

1 pound skinless, boneless chicken breast halves, cut into 1-inch cubes

3 tablespoons vegetable oil, divided

3 celery ribs, sliced

2 green bell peppers, diced

1 onion, chopped

1/2 cup ketchup

1/2 cup lemon juice

1/2 cup crushed pineapple with syrup

1/3 cup packed brown sugar

Direction

In a shallow dish, mix together black pepper, salt, garlic powder and flour.

Roll chicken cubes into the flour mixture to coat.

In a skillet, heat 2 tablespoons of vegetable oil over medium-high heat.

Put in chicken to cook while stirring in hot oil for 8-10 minutes until juices run clear and the center is no longer pink; take it out of the pan and set aside.

In the same skillet, heat 1 tablespoon of vegetable oil over medium heat.

Stir in onion, green peppers and celery into heated oil to cook while stirring for 5 minutes until softened slightly.

Transfer chicken back to the skillet.

In a bowl, mix together brown sugar, pineapple, lemon juice and ketchup; transfer into the skillet and bring to a boil.

Stir vegetables and chicken into the sauce to cook for 2-3 minutes until heated through.

Nutrition Information

Calories: 421 calories;

Sodium: 870

Total Carbohydrate: 49.3

Cholesterol: 65

Protein: 27.4

Total Fat: 13.6

Easy Teriyaki Chicken Brown Rice Dinner

Serving: 4 servings. | Prep: 10mins | Cook: 10mins | Ready in:

Ingredients

1 Tbsp. oil

1 pound boneless skinless chicken breasts, cut into strips

1-1/2 cups water

1/3 cup lite teriyaki sauce

1/2 tsp. garlic powder

2 cups Minute® Brown Rice, uncoooked

2 cups frozen broccoli florets

1/2 cup salted peanuts (optional)

Direction

Heat oil in a big and nonstick pan over medium-high heat. Toss chicken in, cook until cooked through, for 5-7 minutes. Stir while cooking. Add garlic powder, teriyaki sauce, and water. Stir. Let it boil. Add rice, peanuts and broccoli. Stir and put a lid on. Lower heat to Low. Cook for 5 minutes. Take pan away from heat. Rest for 5 minutes. Use a fork to fluff it before serving.

Nutrition Information

Calories:

Cholesterol:

Protein:

Total Fat:

Sodium:

Fiber:

Total Carbohydrate:

Easy And Spicy Thai Basil Chicken With Egg

Serving: 2 | Prep: 10mins | Cook: 15mins | Ready in:
Ingredients

cooking spray

2 eggs

1 1/2 cups cooked white rice

2 Thai chile peppers, or more to taste

2 cloves garlic, peeled, or more to taste

1 chicken breast half, cut into bite-size pieces

2 tablespoons soy sauce

2 tablespoons oyster sauce

1 teaspoon white sugar

14 leaves Thai basil

Direction

Heat a skillet greased with cooking spray over medium heat on the stove; cook eggs in the skillet for about 5 minutes, stirring well, until firm and scrambled. Spoon rice evenly into 2 bowls; add eggs. Grind garlic and Thai chile peppers together in a food processor or with a mortar and pestle. Bring a skillet greased with cooking spray to medium high-heat on the stove; cook and mix pepper-garlic mixture for about 1 minute until garlic turns golden brown and mixture is aromatic. Stir in chicken; sauté for about 3 minutes until chicken is halfway-cooked.

Stir sugar, oyster sauce, and soy sauce into the chicken; keep cooking and stirring for about 3 more minutes until meat is no longer pink inside. Stir in basil for 10 seconds. Turn off the heat; keep stirring until basil is thawed; serve mixture over rice and egg.

Nutrition Information

Calories: 312 calories;

Sodium: 1113

Total Carbohydrate: 38.6

Cholesterol: 218

Protein: 22.6

Total Fat: 6.7

Farmer's Market Corn Toss

Serving: 4 | Prep: 15mins | Cook: 10mins | Ready in:
Ingredients

1 tablespoon olive oil

1 small onion, chopped

1 red bell pepper, chopped

2 ears corn, kernels cut from cob

1 large zucchini, chopped

1/2 cup chopped cooked chicken

1/4 cup chopped fresh parsley

1/4 cup shredded Colby-Monterey Jack cheese, divided

salt and ground black pepper to taste

Direction

Place a large skillet on medium heat; heat olive oil. Add in red pepper and onion; cook while stirring for around 3 minutes, or till softened. Mix in chicken, zucchini and corn; cook while stirring for around 5 minutes, or till all vegetables are crisp-tender. Take the skillet away from the heat.

Sprinkle the vegetable mixture with around half of the cheese and parsley; toss to combine; season with pepper and salt. Transfer the vegetables onto a serving dish; sprinkle the remaining cheese on top.

Nutrition Information

Calories: 164 calories;

Cholesterol: 21

Protein: 9.7

Total Fat: 8.2

Sodium: 95

Total Carbohydrate: 15.2

Fast Sesame Chicken

Serving: 5 servings. | Prep: 30mins | Cook: 0mins | Ready in:

Ingredients

1-1/4 pounds boneless skinless chicken breasts, cubed

2 tablespoons canola oil

1/4 cup soy sauce

1/4 cup sesame seeds

1 large onion, sliced

2 jars (4-1/2 ounces each) sliced mushrooms, drained or 2 cups sliced fresh mushrooms

Direction

Cook chicken with oil in a big skillet until it is not pink anymore. Stir in sesame seeds and soy sauce, then cook and stir on moderate heat about 5 minutes.

Use a slotted spoon to take chicken out of skillet, then set aside and keep it warm. Sauté mushrooms and onion together in the same skillet until onion is softened. Turn the chicken back to pan and heat through.

Nutrition Information

Calories: 272 calories

Sodium: 474mg sodium

Fiber: 2g fiber)

Total Carbohydrate: 8g carbohydrate (0 sugars

Cholesterol: 73mg cholesterol

Protein: 31g protein. Diabetic Exchanges: 3 lean meat

Total Fat: 13g fat (0 saturated fat)

Favorite Sweet And Sour Chicken

Serving: 4 servings. | Prep: 20mins | Cook: 15mins | Ready in:

Ingredients

1 tablespoon plus 2 teaspoons reduced-sodium soy sauce, divided

1 tablespoon sherry or reduced-sodium chicken broth

1/2 teaspoon salt

1/2 teaspoon garlic powder

1/2 teaspoon ground ginger

1 pound boneless skinless chicken breasts, cut into 1-inch cubes

1 can (20 ounces) unsweetened pineapple chunks

2 tablespoons plus 1/3 cup cornstarch, divided

2 tablespoons sugar

1/4 cup cider vinegar

1/4 cup ketchup

1 tablespoon canola oil

2 cups hot cooked rice

Direction

Mix the sherry or broth, ginger, 1 tbsp. of soy sauce, garlic powder, and salt in a large resealable plastic bag. Place the chicken inside the bag. Seal the bag, flipping it until the chicken is well coated. Place it inside the fridge for half an hour.

Drain the pineapple and reserve its juices. Put the pineapple aside. You can add enough water to the juice until it measures 1 cup. Mix 2 tbsp. of cornstarch, pineapple juice mixture, and sugar in a small bowl until smooth. Mix in the remaining soy sauce, ketchup, and vinegar; put aside.

Drain the chicken, discarding the marinade. In a large resealable plastic bag, place the remaining cornstarch and add the chicken, few pieces at a time. Shake the bag until the chicken is coated. Coat the wok or large nonstick skillet with cooking spray. Stir-fry the chicken in oil until it is no longer pink. Remove from the heat and keep it warm.

Whisk the pineapple juice mixture before adding it into the pan; boil. Cook and stir the mixture for 2 minutes until thick. Add the reserved pineapple and chicken. Heat the mixture through and serve it together with the rice.

Nutrition Information
Calories: 428 calories
Protein: 26g protein.
Total Fat: 6g fat (1g saturated fat)
Sodium: 571mg sodium
Fiber: 2g fiber)
Total Carbohydrate: 65g carbohydrate (24g sugars
Cholesterol: 63mg cholesterol

Fiery Pepper Chicken

Serving: 4 | Prep: 20mins | Cook: 15mins | Ready in:
Ingredients
1 teaspoon Chinese cooking wine
1/2 teaspoon salt
1/2 pound boneless chicken, cut into 1/2 inch cubes

1/4 cup cornstarch, or as needed
3 cups peanut oil for frying
4 cloves garlic, minced
1 tablespoon minced fresh ginger root
2 green onions, julienned
2 long, green chilies - cut into 1/2-inch pieces
2 cups dried chilies, chopped
2 tablespoons Szechuan peppercorns
2 teaspoons soy sauce
2 teaspoons Chinese cooking wine
1/2 teaspoon white sugar
1/2 teaspoon salt

Direction

Combine 1/2 teaspoon salt and 1 teaspoon cooking wine in a bowl and stir them together. Add the chicken and coat it by stirring it in. Leave it to marinate for 2-3 minutes. Combine the marinated chicken and cornstarch in a big sealable plastic bag then shake it to coat the chicken.

In a big cooking pan or wok, heat the peanut oil on high heat. Fry the chicken for 7-10 minutes in the oil until the edges start to get crisp. Move the chicken to a plate lined with paper towels to drain. Discard the oil, leaving 2 tablespoons.

Reheat the remaining 2 tablespoons of oil in the wok on medium-high heat. Cook the garlic, green onions and ginger in the oil for a minute until fragrant. Add the green chilies, Szechuan peppercorns, and crushed dried chilies then continue to fry for another 20 seconds. Put the chicken back to the wok and add 2 teaspoons cooking wine, soy sauce, 1/2 teaspoon salt, and sugar while stirring until they are well blended together. Turn the heat and off serve right away.

Nutrition Information

Calories: 336 calories;

Sodium: 807

Total Carbohydrate: 26.7

Cholesterol: 35

Protein: 15.9

Total Fat: 19.5

Freezer Friendly Thai Chicken

Serving: 6 | Prep: 20mins | Cook: 10mins | Ready in:
Ingredients

1/2 cup unsweetened light coconut milk

1/4 cup reduced-sodium soy sauce

1/4 cup creamy peanut butter

5 teaspoons sriracha sauce

1 tablespoon lime juice

4 1/2 cups cubed cooked chicken breast

2 cups thinly sliced red bell pepper

1 cup thinly bias-sliced carrots

1 cup fresh snow pea pods

5 1/3 tablespoons sesame oil

Direction

In a big bowl, combine lime juice, sriracha, peanut butter, soy sauce, and coconut milk. Add snow peas, carrots, red bell pepper, and chicken; mix to blend.

In a wok or a big frying pan, heat sesame oil over medium-low heat. Add the chicken mixture, stir and cook for 10 minutes until fully heated.

Nutrition Information

Calories: 378 calories;

Total Fat: 22.6

Sodium: 676

Total Carbohydrate: 8.6

Cholesterol: 81

Protein: 34.7

www.ingramcontent.com/pod-product-compliance
Lightning Source LLC
Chambersburg PA
CBHW071441070526
44578CB00001B/178